Essential genetics

A course book

Lynn Burnet

CAMBRIDGE
UNIVERSITY PRESS

PUBLISHED BY THE PRESS SYNDICATE OF THE UNIVERSITY OF CAMBRIDGE
The Pitt Building, Trumpington Street, Cambridge CB2 1RP, United Kingdom

CAMBRIDGE UNIVERSITY PRESS
The Edinburgh Building, Cambridge CB2 2RU, United Kingdom
40 West 20th Street, New York, NY 10011–4211, USA
10 Stamford Road, Oakleigh, Melbourne 3166, Australia

First published 1986
Seventh printing 1997

Printed in the United Kingdom at the University Press, Cambridge

A catalogue record for this book is available from the British Library

ISBN 0 521 31380 5 paperback

Acknowledgements

I would like first of all to thank my husband Dr Barrie Burnet for his advice, assistance and encouragement throughout the preparation of the manuscript and for drawing the diagrams of *Drosophila* used in chapter 2. I thank other members of the Genetics Department at Sheffield University, Professor Alan Roper and Dr Morris Grindle together with Drs Philip Greig, Roger Kemp and Peter Screen for their comments on the manuscript. These were greatly appreciated if not always acted upon and full responsibility for any errors remaining is mine alone. Thanks are also due to the sixth-form pupils at King Edward VII School, Sheffield, who have worked through many of the problems and especially to A. Bunting, A. Edwards, C. Hill and C. Rick for their constructive criticisms on the text; to Mr B. Taylor and Dr J. Gallimore and sixth-formers at Kesteven and Grantham Girls School and to Mr D. Gregory and sixth-formers at The King's School, Grantham, who worked through the test questions. I am very grateful to the Goldsmiths' Company for financial support, to the City of Sheffield Education Department for a term's secondment and to the Master and Fellows of St Catharine's College, Cambridge, for their provision of a most congenial environment in which to complete the manuscript during my tenure of a Schoolteacher Fellow Commonership.

Contents

Preface

This book has been written primarily for students of biological sciences at A-level or its equivalent. It will also be of value to undergraduates reading any of the biological or social sciences where a knowledge of basic genetics is required. It is hoped too that practical breeders of animals and plants will find enlightenment in its pages.

It has not been possible in a short book to deal adequately with all aspects of genetics but my aim has been to provide a course in transmission genetics, that is, the way in which genes are inherited. It is assumed that the reader has knowledge of the structure of DNA and its role in protein synthesis and also of the principles of mitosis and meiosis. These topics are normally taught before transmission genetics in advanced-level courses in biology. Anyone interested only in the consequences of crossing one variety of animal or plant with another can omit sections 1.5, 2.1, 2.2, 3.3 and 5.2.

Of all biological topics, genetics is often regarded as one of the most difficult and some of the reasons for this can be identified. There is a special vocabulary associated with the subject and it also requires logical thinking, the use of symbols and some mathematics. From the teacher's point of view, a large amount of material must be presented in an orderly sequence in a short period of time. Another problem is that the use of genetical symbols and terminology is inconsistent amongst textbooks and examination boards. I hope that this book will show that genetics is not difficult and will provide a reference for the standardization of the use of genetical terms in schools.

To the teacher

This course book is a teaching aid which provides a logical progression through transmission genetics. The questions at the end of each chapter are graded for difficulty and allow practice in handling the concepts introduced in the chapter. There should be sufficient problems to satisfy the needs of those studying any of the biological sciences and to stretch the most able students. The questions are instructive; most of the data have been taken from published research and the information is factual even where the problem has been contrived. Wherever possible, examples have been chosen from familiar animals and plants as well as humans. The answers are explained in full so that students may learn from their mistakes.

The problems at the end of the book test a student's ability to recognize the concepts required for their solution, simulating conditions encountered in an examination. Some of these problems are admittedly difficult but none demands any more knowledge than can be gained from the text. The answers are less explanatory and have been printed in such a way that they can be removed if desired, using a craft knife.

As the science of genetics has grown, so has its vocabulary. Over the years, the use and meaning of some genetical terms has changed and confusion over terms is an unnecessary source of difficulty. In this book, I have made a conscious effort to define terms precisely and to use them in a consistent manner according to their modern meaning. This has not always been easy because even professional geneticists are sometimes guilty of inconsistency. Nevertheless, it is important that a student who is trying to understand principles should not be confused by semantics.

The same comments can be made about the use of genetical symbols. Different notations are in use according to the organisms studied although the principles are the same in each case. I have used a single system throughout in the belief that once this is mastered, there should be no difficulty in adjusting to another system later.

To the student

You will find that there is a large amount of information in this small book. To aid your understanding, there are questions within the text which are intended to make you stop, consider and consolidate what you have just read. Avoid the temptation to skip these questions; they are an essential part of the developing argument.

In my experience many students take fright when they see genetics problems which hint at mathematics but the mathematical ability required is minimal. Explanation of the methods is presented in very easy steps and I have not gone beyond what is required to solve the problems in this book.

Many of the problems are genuine ones which concerned the investigators who helped to build the body of knowledge called genetics. Others are problems which might well be encountered by horticulturalists, gardeners and animal breeders. If you are one of these, an elementary knowledge of genetics could save a great deal of time.

If you are studying independently of a teacher, the text should provide you with a comprehensive course in Mendelian genetics. You can be selective in the problems you attempt but an A-level student should be able to solve at least two-thirds of the problems at the end of each chapter. The final three or four problems following chapters 3, 5 and 6 should be attempted if you feel the need for a greater challenge.

The test questions are mixed, both in the ideas involved and in the level of difficulty which ranges from moderately easy to difficult. Even these can be solved if you have a thorough understanding of the text. If you like solving problems, you'll enjoy genetics.

1 Monohybrid inheritance (1)

1.1 Mendel's experiments and conclusions

The laws of heredity were worked out by the Austrian monk, Gregor Mendel, and published in 1866. His contribution to genetics is so important that the adjective 'Mendelian' is now used to describe the kind of experiments he did and the principles he formulated.

Mendel was not the first to carry out breeding experiments but he was the first to analyse the results numerically and thereby discover certain consistencies which he explained in terms of 'hereditary factors'. He made a careful choice of organism with which to do his breeding experiments. The garden pea, *Pisum sativum*, satisfied his requirements for the following reasons.

(a) There exist many easily recognizable, distinct forms or varieties.
(b) The flowers are normally self fertilized but it is possible to remove the stamens from a flower before they are mature and to pollinate the stigma with pollen from a different variety.
(c) The plants resulting from cross fertilization are fully viable and fertile.
(d) The plants are easy to cultivate.
(e) The one year life cycle is short enough to be able to collect data from several generations.

Mendel obtained 34 varieties of peas and chose from them a number which showed distinct, contrasting forms (Table 1). Throughout this

Table 1 *The varieties of the garden pea used by Mendel*

Character	Trait
Form of ripe seed	Smooth or wrinkled
Colour of cotyledons	Yellow or green
Colour of testa	White or grey
Colour of flower	White or purple
Form of ripe pods	Inflated or constricted
Colour of unripe pods	Green or yellow
Position of flowers	Axial (distributed along the stem) or terminal (bunched at the top of the stem)
Length of stem	Tall (2 m) or short (less than 0·5 m)

book, the terms 'character' and 'trait' will be used in the restricted sense explained in Table 1. Other textbooks tend to use the terms interchangeably.

Mendel was quite aware that characters often had more than two traits but he deliberately restricted his investigations. He took each character in turn and cross fertilized plants which showed the two alternative traits. For instance, he took several white flowered plants and removed the stamens from all the young flowers. Then he dusted the stigmas of the white flowers with pollen taken from purple flowers. He also did the **reciprocal cross** in which he removed stamens from purple flowers and pollinated them with pollen from white flowers. With all the pairs of traits he used, he found that in the generation resulting from the cross fertilizations (called the first filial or **F₁ generation**) the plants all showed the same trait. All the offspring were like one of the parents and were not intermediate in appearance. Furthermore, the appearance of the F₁ generation was the same regardless of which plant bore the seeds. An example is illustrated in Table 2.

Table 2 *The results of two reciprocal crosses*

Female parent axial flowers	Male parent terminal flowers	Female parent terminal flowers	Male parent axial flowers
\	/	\	/
Cross fertilized		Cross fertilized	
↓		↓	
F₁		F₁	
axial flowers		axial flowers	

1.1.1 A white female mouse was mated to a black male. What is the reciprocal cross?

Mendel called the trait which was shown by the F₁ generation the **dominant** trait. The other he called the **recessive** trait because it seems to recede out of sight in this generation. But, as later experiments demonstrated, it can reappear in subsequent generations. Mendel found the following relationships:

Dominant trait	Recessive trait
Smooth seed	Wrinkled seed
Yellow cotyledons	Green cotyledons
Grey testa	White testa
Purple flowers	White flowers
Inflated pods	Constricted pods
Green unripe pods	Yellow unripe pods
Axial flowers	Terminal flowers
Tall stem	Short stem

Figure 1 *Mendel's experiment with smooth and wrinkled seeds*

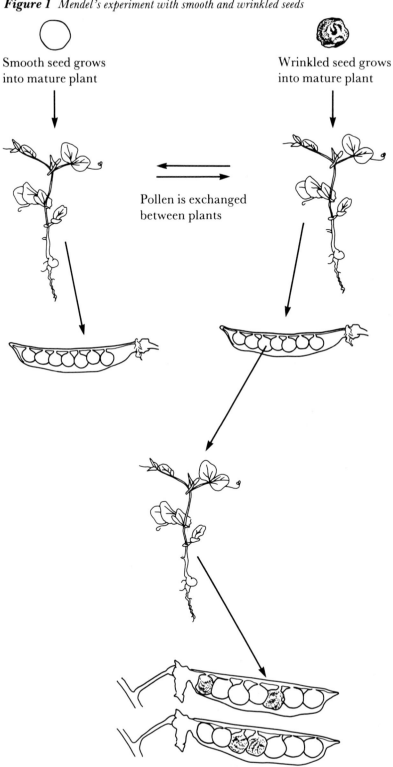

Smooth seed grows
into mature plant

Wrinkled seed grows
into mature plant

Pollen is exchanged
between plants

Regardless of which plant
bears them, all the seeds
resulting from this cross are
smooth. These are the F_1
seeds.

These smooth seeds grow
into mature plants (the F_1
generation). Self
fertilization results in the
formation of the F_2 seeds.
¾ of them are smooth and
¼ are wrinkled. Both kinds
occur in the same pod.

Plants of the F_1 generation were then **selfed** (allowed to self fertilize) and the progeny were collected. In this second generation (called the second filial or **F_2 generation**) some plants showed the dominant trait and some showed the recessive trait. For each character, Mendel looked at about one thousand F_2 plants and counted the numbers having the dominant and the recessive trait. For the seed characters, he was able to count many more individuals because he did not have to grow the seeds in order to find out what the plants would look like. The pods on the F_1 plants bear the seeds of the F_2 generation. Mendel's breeding scheme is illustrated in Figure 1. From 253 F_1 plants he collected 7324 seeds. Of these, 5474 were smooth and 1850 were wrinkled. $5474 \div 1850 = 2.96$, so the ratio of smooth to wrinkled is $2.96 : 1$. Whichever character he investigated, he found this ratio of approximately **3 dominant trait : 1 recessive trait** in the F_2 generation.

Next, plants of the F_2 generation were selfed to produce the F_3 generation. Those F_2 plants showing the recessive trait had F_3 offspring all of which also showed the recessive trait. The F_2 plants showing the dominant trait were found to be of two kinds. One-third of them yielded F_3 offspring which always showed the dominant trait. The other two-thirds yielded F_3 offspring which had either the dominant or the recessive trait, again in the ratio $3 : 1$. The crosses are illustrated in Table 3. In this

Table 3 *The results of Mendel's experiments with three generations of peas*

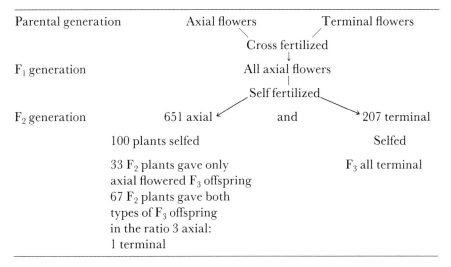

example, all the terminal flowered F_2 plants had only terminal flowered offspring. One-third of the axial flowered F_2 plants had only axial flowered offspring. A plant which, when selfed, has offspring only like itself is said to be **pure breeding** or **true breeding**. There are three different types of plant in the F_2 generation and they occur in the following proportions:

$\frac{1}{4}$ pure breeding for the dominant trait	$\frac{1}{2}$ not pure breeding but also showing the dominant trait	$\frac{1}{4}$ pure breeding for the recessive trait

This is a ratio of **1 : 2 : 1**.

It was from such results that Mendel worked out his first law of inheritance. His most important conclusion was that the units of inheritance remain as separate 'particles' when they are passed from generation to generation. They are not changed or 'diluted' and although their effects may be hidden, the particles themselves are passed on unchanged. This is called the idea of **particulate inheritance**.

1.2   Particulate inheritance explained in modern terms

Each character is controlled by a gene. Genes can exist in alternative forms called **alleles** which control the alternative traits of a character. The genes are the 'particles' which are transmitted unchanged from one generation to the next. A gene is represented by a symbol, say the letter 'A'. Two alleles, being different forms of the gene, are known by alternative forms of the symbol, e.g. *A* and *a*. If *A* represents the allele for the dominant trait and *a* represents the allele for the recessive trait, then *A* and *a* are called the dominant and recessive alleles respectively. Crosses like those described above, which take account of only one pair of alleles, are called **monohybrid crosses**.

Each diploid organism carries two alleles of each gene. If the two alleles are the same, the organism is said to be **homozygous** (Greek *homos* means 'the same'). If it is homozygous for the dominant allele, it is called **homozygous dominant** (represented *AA*). If it is homozygous for the recessive allele, it is **homozygous recessive** (represented *aa*). Both types can be called **homozygotes**. A homozygote is **pure breeding** because if it is selfed or crossed to a similar homozygote, all the offspring will be the same as the parent(s). If the organism carries two different alleles, it is said to be **heterozygous** (represented *Aa*). Such a plant or animal is called a **heterozygote** (Greek *heteros* means 'different').

The words homozygous and heterozygous describe an individual's genetic make-up, i.e. its **genotype**, whereas its outward appearance is called its **phenotype** (Greek *phainomai* means 'I appear'). Colour, form, physiology and behaviour are all aspects of the phenotype. The homozygous recessive genotype (*aa*) shows the recessive trait while both the homozygous dominant genotype (*AA*) and the heterozygote (*Aa*) show the dominant trait. Note that one does not speak of the 'heterozygous dominant' since there is only one kind of heterozygote.

Mendel's first law is known as the **Law of Segregation** and, in modern terms, states that when an organism forms gametes, only one of a pair of alleles enters each gamete. (In animals, the gametes are eggs and sperm; in plants, they are nuclei in the ovules and pollen grains.) In our example, the gametes can have either A or a but never both. At gamete formation by meiosis, the alleles segregate (separate) from each other (see section 1.5). Each homozygote can produce only one type of gamete since it carries only one type of allele. Heterozygotes yield two types of gametes in equal proportions, half carrying A and the other half carrying a.

Table 4 shows again Mendel's experiment with the flower position character and introduces a method of showing all possible combinations of alleles in the zygotes of the F_2 generation. This grid is called a **Punnett square** after one of the early geneticists, R. C. Punnett, who first used the method. The alleles from each sex and the probabilities with which they occur are given above the grid and at the left-hand side. The possible genotypes of the zygotes are shown within the grid. The probabilities of obtaining the zygote genotypes are calculated by multiplying together the probability of occurrence of each of the alleles involved. (A more detailed explanation of probability will be found in section 2.6.)

Table 4 *Inheritance of flower position*

Parental phenotype	Axial flowers	Terminal flowers
Parental genotype	AA	aa
Parental gametes	All A	All a

Cross fertilized
↓

F$_1$ genotype	Aa
F$_1$ phenotype	All axial flowers
F$_1$ gametes	$\frac{1}{2}A$ and $\frac{1}{2}a$

↓

F$_1$ plants self fertilized

F$_2$ genotypes shown in the table

Gametes from F$_1$ males

		$\frac{1}{2}A$	$\frac{1}{2}a$
Gametes from F$_1$ females	$\frac{1}{2}A$	$\frac{1}{4}AA$	$\frac{1}{4}Aa$
	$\frac{1}{2}a$	$\frac{1}{4}Aa$	$\frac{1}{4}aa$

F$_2$ phenotypes $\frac{1}{4}AA + \frac{1}{4}Aa + \frac{1}{4}Aa = \frac{3}{4}$ axial flowers (shaded)
$\frac{1}{4}aa = \frac{1}{4}$ terminal flowers

The F$_1$ plants are all heterozygous but because the allele for axial flowers is dominant to the allele for terminal flowers, the F$_1$ plants have axial flowers. Three quarters of the F_2 plants have the dominant phenotype but some are homozygous and some are heterozygous. Mendel demonstrated this when he showed that some of the F_2 generation were pure breeding and some were not. The ratios of the various types of F_2 progeny are

Phenotypic ratio   **3 dominant trait : 1 recessive trait**

Genotypic ratio   **1 homozygous dominant : 2 heterozygotes : 1 homozygous recessive**

1.2.1   From the list of items below, select all those which are
(i) phenotypes, (ii) genotypes, (iii) homozygous, (iv) homozygous recessive, (v) heterozygous, (vi) pure breeding.
A *Ss*   B *AA*   C *Ww*   D tall   E *TT*   F *Tt*   G *ss*
H *Pp*   I *Aa*   J purple flowers   K *BB*   L *pp*

1.3   *The standard monohybrid cross*

Monohybrid crosses are those which involve a single character which is controlled by one gene with at least two alleles. The simplest monohybrid cross involves one character with two traits, one trait being dominant to the other. Put another way, it involves one gene with two alleles, one

Table 5 *A monohybrid cross in mice*

Parental phenotype	Grey	Albino (white)
Parental genotype	*GG*	*gg*
Parental gametes	All *G*	All *g*

Cross fertilized
↓

F_1 genotype	*Gg*
F_1 phenotype	All grey
F_1 gametes	$\frac{1}{2}G$ and $\frac{1}{2}g$

↓

F_1 animals interbred

F_2 genotypes shown in the table

Gametes from F_1 males

		$\frac{1}{2}G$	$\frac{1}{2}g$
Gametes from F_1 females	$\frac{1}{2}G$	$\frac{1}{4}GG$	$\frac{1}{4}Gg$
	$\frac{1}{2}g$	$\frac{1}{4}Gg$	$\frac{1}{4}gg$

F_2 phenotypes $\frac{3}{4}$ grey (shaded) and $\frac{1}{4}$ albino allele being dominant to the other. After the rediscovery of Mendel's work in 1900, investigators soon found that inheritance in animals followed the same laws as inheritance in pea plants. Table 5 shows a standard monohybrid cross in mice. Unlike pea plants, mice cannot fertilize themselves and so the F_2 generation is obtained by interbreeding the F_1 animals.

1.3.1   What is the phenotypic ratio in the F_2 generation shown in Table 5?

1.3.2   What is the genotypic ratio?

1.4   The monohybrid backcross or testcross

In the example above, the grey F_2 progeny are either homozygous dominant (GG) or heterozygous (Gg). The exact genotype is not apparent from the phenotype. The genotype of the albino can only be gg. The way to discover an unknown genotype is by carrying out a further cross known as the **testcross**. A testcross always involves crossing the unknown genotype to the homozygous recessive. This is the genotype of one of the parents in the standard monohybrid cross and so it is also known as a **backcross**. The outcomes of two possible crosses are shown in Table 6.

Table 6 *Expected results from two testcrosses*

Parental phenotype	Grey	Albino	Grey	Albino
Parental genotype	GG	gg	Gg	gg
Parental gametes	All G	All g	$\frac{1}{2}G$ and $\frac{1}{2}g$	All g
Fertilization				
Backcross progeny: Genotype		Gg	$\frac{1}{2}Gg$ and $\frac{1}{2}gg$	
Phenotype		All grey	$\frac{1}{2}$ grey and $\frac{1}{2}$ albino	

If the unknown genotype is GG, all the backcross progeny will inherit a G from that parent and will show the dominant trait, grey. If the unknown genotype is Gg, each of its offspring has a 1 in 2 chance of receiving a G and the same chance of receiving a g. They will all inherit a g from the albino parent. Therefore, on average, the offspring of a heterozygote and a homozygous recessive show a ratio of **1 hetero-zygote:1 homozygous recessive**. If even a single offspring in a testcross shows the recessive phenotype, we know that both of its parents must carry a recessive allele and therefore the unknown genotype must be heterozygous.

1.5 *The physical basis of the Law of Segregation*

By 1916 it was known that genes are located in a linear sequence along chromosomes (see section 5.6). Diploid organisms have two complete sets of chromosomes in each cell and therefore have two copies of each gene. The position of a gene in relation to other genes on the chromosome is known as the **gene locus** and it is often more convenient to speak of a gene locus when it is of no consequence which particular allele occupies it. In haploid cells, each gene locus is represented only once, since there is only one set of chromosomes. Haploid organisms cannot be described as being either homozygous or heterozygous and there is no question of dominance or recessivity. This makes the genetics of haploid organisms (e.g. bacteria) quite straightforward. In polyploids (see section 5.7), each set of chromosomes and therefore each locus is represented three, four or more times, making the study of heredity in these organisms correspondingly more complicated.

This book is concerned with heredity in diploids where each chromosome is represented twice in each cell. The two copies have the same sequence of genes although the chromosomes are not necessarily identical because the alleles at each locus may be different. The two chromosomes carrying the same gene loci are called **homologues**; they are said to be **homologous**. Thus in the heterozygote, *Aa*, one homologue carries allele *A* and the other carries allele *a* at the same gene locus. One of the homologues in each cell is a copy of the original chromosome which was donated to the zygote by the male parent and is known as the **paternal homologue**. Its partner is a copy of one of the chromosomes which came from the female gamete and is known as the **maternal homologue**. Both homologues are fully functional in the cell regardless of the sex of the organism.

In order to explain his results, Mendel assumed that the 'factors' (alleles) determining each trait were present in pairs in the parent plants but segregated at gamete formation such that each gamete received only one of the factors. Later observations on the behaviour of chromosomes in meiosis provided a physical parallel and indeed were taken as evidence that the segregating factors were situated on the chromosomes (see section 5.6). It is assumed that the student understands the principles of gamete formation by meiosis. Figure 2 shows the behaviour of only one pair of homologues and concentrates on the relationships between alleles, chromosomes and Mendel's first law.

No attempt is made here to describe the events of meiosis but it might be helpful to clarify the terms 'chromosome' and 'chromatid'. A *chromosome* is one long molecule of DNA arranged on a framework of protein molecules. (The latter are not thought to carry any genetic information.) In the interphase prior to the first division of the nucleus, the DNA replicates (makes an exact copy of itself) and each replica also becomes

Figure 2 *Segregation of alleles A and a during meiosis in a heterozygote*

(i) During **interphase** prior to meiosis, each homologue replicates itself.

(a) Allele **A**   Gene locus 'A'   (b)

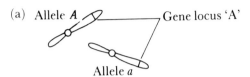

Allele *a*

Homologues before replication.
Gene locus 'A' is represented
twice in the nucleus.

Homologues after replication.
Gene locus 'A' is now
represented four times
because each homologue
now consists of two identical
chromatids.

(ii)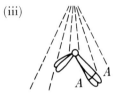

At **prophase I** of meiosis, the homologues pair
with each other, gene for gene. (Chiasmata
have been omitted. See section 5.2.)

(iii)

At **anaphase I** the homologues separate and go
to opposite poles of the spindle.
The alleles *A* and *a* have now separated or
segregated. (But see section 5.2.)

(iv)

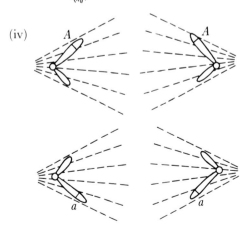

At **anaphase II** the
chromatids separate and
at **telophase II** each new
nucleus contains one of
these chromatids (which we
should now call a chromosome).

(v)

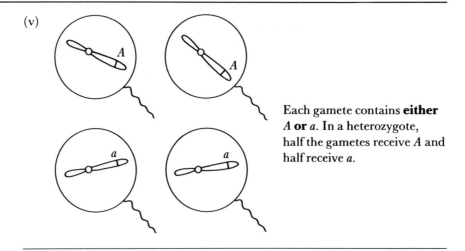

Each gamete contains **either** *A* **or** *a*. In a heterozygote, half the gametes receive *A* and half receive *a*.

associated with protein. The two replicas shorten in preparation for cell division and become visible under the microscope, lying alongside each other and joined at a constriction (represented by a circle in the diagrams) called the *centromere*. Each replica is called a *chromatid*. The chromatids are identical to the original chromosome which replicated. To draw an analogy, chromatids are like twin sisters. When they are considered in relation to each other, they are called chromatids ('sisters'), and when each is being considered alone, it is called a chromosome ('a girl'). A chromatid is a chromosome, just as a sister is a girl. The chromatids pull apart at anaphase and at telophase, the name chromosome is used again. It is only the name and not the structure which has changed. The analogy with twin sisters is a pertinent one because chromosome replicas are often called sister chromatids.

Figure 2 illustrates segregation in a heterozygote but the chromosomes separate in just the same way in a homozygote. Here, the homologues carry identical alleles, so at this gene locus each of its gametes possesses the same kind of allele.

The diagrams also make it evident that a male's gametes may carry chromosomes which are copies of those received from his mother. Similarly, a female may pass on copies of chromosomes which came from her father. This helps to explain an observation with which we are all familiar, the resemblance between a boy and his maternal grandfather or between a girl and her paternal grandmother. Mendel demonstrated quite clearly that whichever kind of plant donated the pollen or bore the seeds, the same results were obtained, i.e. there was no difference between reciprocal crosses. This is because any allele can be carried and passed on by either sex. There are exceptions which will be explained in chapter 4.

1.6 Summary

After breeding experiments with the garden pea, Mendel came to the conclusion that each of the characters he investigated was under the control of two factors which we now call alleles. Each plant contains either two similar or two different alleles and they are passed on, unchanged, to the next generation. The alleles segregate during meiosis and come together again at random when gametes unite at fertilization.

Subsequent work on inheritance in other plants and in animals has shown that it is consistent with the basic laws discovered by Mendel. Such inheritance is described as 'Mendelian' and the first of the two basic laws, the Law of Segregation, is explained in this chapter.

One of the consequences of the Law of Segregation is that the ratio of different types in the progeny of a cross can be predicted. These ratios are summarized below.

$3:1$ phenotypic ratio from $Aa \times Aa$ where A is dominant to a. The ratio is 3 dominant trait : 1 recessive trait.

$1:2:1$ genotypic ratio from the same cross. The ratio is 1 AA : 2 Aa : 1 aa.

$1:1$ phenotypic and genotypic ratio from $Aa \times aa$ (a testcross). The ratio is 1 dominant trait (Aa) : 1 recessive trait (aa).

Key words

	Section		Section
allele	1.2	homozygous recessive	1.2
backcross	1.4	Law of Segregation	1.2
character	1.1	maternal homologue	1.5
chromatid	1.5	monohybrid cross	1.2
chromosome	1.5	particulate inheritance	1.1
dominant	1.1	paternal homologue	1.5
F_1 generation	1.1	phenotype	1.2
F_2 generation	1.1	pure breeding	1.1
gene locus	1.5	recessive	1.1
genotype	1.2	reciprocal cross	1.1
heterozygote, heterozygous	1.2	selfed	1.1
homologue, homologous	1.5	testcross	1.4
homozygote, homozygous	1.2	trait	1.1
homozygous dominant	1.2	true breeding	1.1

Answers

1.1.1   Black female × white male.

1.2.1   (i) D, J;   (ii) A, B, C, E, F, G, H, I, K, L;   (iii) B, E, G, K, L;
(iv) G, L;   (v) A, C, F, H, I;   (vi) B, E, G, K, L.
D and J could be homozygous (pure breeding) or heterozygous. It is not possible to tell from the phenotype.

1.3.1   3 grey : 1 albino.

1.3.2   1 *GG* : 2 *Gg* : 1 *gg*.

PROBLEMS

1   In maize, starchy seed is dominant to sugary. Two pure breeding plants are crossed, one grown from a starchy seed and the other grown from a sugary seed.
(a) What is the phenotype of the F_1 seeds?
(b) These F_1 seeds grew into mature plants and were allowed to self fertilize. What is the expected ratio of starchy to sugary seeds in the cobs borne on the F_1 plants?

2   Mendel crossed pure breeding plants having green unripe pods with pure breeding plants having yellow unripe pods. The F_1 plants had green pods. He allowed these to self fertilize and collected 580 F_2 plants. How many of these would be expected to have green pods and how many yellow pods?

3   A variety of pure breeding 'hooded' sweet peas was crossed with a pure breeding 'erect' variety (see Figure 3). The F_1 plants were allowed to self fertilize. The F_2 generation consisted of 192 erect and 64 hooded. What was the phenotype of the F_1 plants?

Figure 3 *Types of sweet pea*

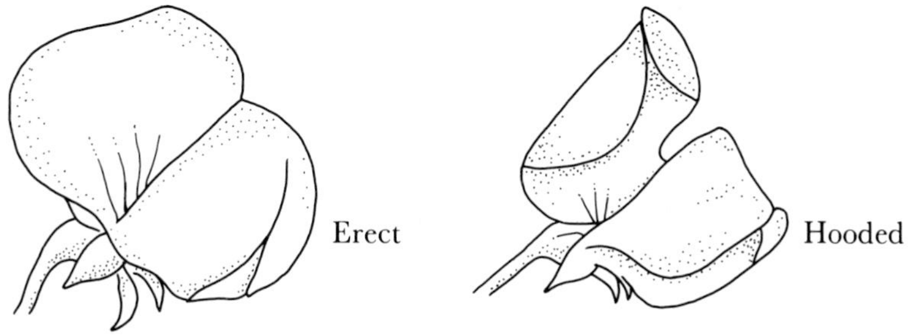

Erect   Hooded

4   Mendel crossed pea plants homozygous for the allele for inflated pods with plants homozygous for the allele for constricted pods and allowed the F_1 plants to self fertilize. He collected 1181 F_2 plants of which 882 had inflated pods. What is the ratio of inflated:constricted in the F_2 generation?

5   The snail *Cepaea nemoralis* has either a plain or a banded shell. A naturalist captured two immature unbanded specimens and kept them until maturity when they mated and produced a total of 34 unbanded and 12 banded progeny.
(a) Using suitable symbols give the genotypes of the two unbanded parents.
(b) Give the genotypes of the unbanded progeny.

6   A gene causing the disease cystic fibrosis in humans is recessive to its normal allele. A man is heterozygous for cystic fibrosis. Does he suffer from the disease?

7   In guinea pigs, short hair is dominant to Angora (long hair). A heterozygous animal was mated to a homozygous recessive.
(a) What are the phenotypes of these animals?
(b) Using suitable symbols, give their genotypes.
(c) What proportion of their litter are expected to be Angora?

8   Two agouti (brown) gerbils were mated and some of the progeny were black. If the same two animals were mated on several occasions, approximately what ratio of agouti to black would be expected in their progeny?

9   Two tomato plants were crossed together and the seeds were collected. When they germinated, about one-quarter of them produced seedlings which grew slowly into very small plants while the rest grew normally. These normal sized progeny were then selfed. What proportion of the normal sized plants would be expected to have some small sized progeny?

10   Lincoln Red cattle are entirely red. Hereford cattle have a white face. The white face is due to a dominant allele for which the Hereford breed is homozygous. A farmer has a herd of Lincoln Red cows and Larry, a Lincoln Red bull. Larry was allowed to mate with the cows but died of exhaustion before he had fertilized the whole herd. The farmer borrowed a neighbour's Hereford bull called Herbert, to finish Larry's job.
(a) When the calves were born, the farmer found he could distinguish between Larry's and Herbert's offspring. How?
(b) He kept one of Herbert's male offspring to replace Larry. When this bull was mated to the Lincoln Red cows, what would be the phenotypes of the calves and in what proportions?

11 The Japanese waltzing mouse has a peculiar behaviour pattern. It spins round as if chasing after its tail. A homozygous normal mouse was mated to a homozygous waltzing mouse. The F_1 mice were all normal. An F_1 animal was crossed with a waltzer. What would be the expected proportion of normal to waltzers in their progeny?

12 'White forelock', a patch of white hair at the front of the head, is a dominant condition in humans. A woman with white forelock married a normal man and had a daughter with white forelock. The daughter also married a normal man. What is the likelihood that her first child will have white forelock?

2 Monohybrid inheritance (2)

2.1 The origin of new alleles

The first two sections in this chapter assume that the student has knowledge of the structure of deoxyribonucleic acid (DNA) and its role in protein synthesis. Although such knowledge is not essential in order to understand Mendelian genetics, some idea of what genes are and how they work certainly aids comprehension.

A gene is a length of DNA which has a specific function. Not all genes specify a polypeptide; some code for ribosomal or transfer RNA while others have a regulatory function, influencing whether or not other genes are active. Whatever their functions, all genes are inherited in the same way. (There are exceptions. Mitochondria contain DNA and their genes follow the inheritance of the cytoplasm. Such inheritance is called cytoplasmic or non-Mendelian inheritance.)

A gene is normally located at a certain position on a certain chromosome in all cells of all organisms of the same species. This site is called the gene locus (see also section 1.5). The gene which occupies a particular locus will have a sequence of bases which performs a function such as the specification of a polypeptide. This polypeptide may in turn affect the appearance of the organism. As an example, take the gene locus called *white* in the fruit fly *Drosophila*. The commonly occurring sequence of bases at this locus is thought to code for a protein involved in the development of eye colour. Flies caught in the wild have red eyes so red is known as the **wild type** eye colour. There exists another sequence of bases at the *white* locus which fails to produce the necessary protein. No pigment accumulates in the eyes so they are white. Each sequence of bases at a locus is called an allele (see also section 1.2). The one which produces the normal red eye is called the wild type allele, which can be regarded as the original sequence. A change in the sequence has produced another allele, known as *white*. Written in italics, *white* is both the name of a locus and the name of an allele which occurs there. The name is taken from the phenotypic effect of the allele and does not of course describe the allele itself. The name of a recessive allele should always be written with a lower case initial letter while a dominant allele is written with a capital initial letter. In this book, the symbols representing alleles are printed in italics and the symbol for the gene locus is printed in inverted commas, for example, *B* and *b* are alleles at the 'B' locus. The term wild type is neither italicized nor written with a capital letter even when it is the dominant allele. It is the term used to describe the 'normal' allele at any gene locus and in any organism.

The process of changing the sequence of bases in DNA is called **mutation**. Every new allele originates by mutation of a pre-existing one and can be called a **mutant allele**. An individual such as the white eyed *Drosophila*, which shows the effects of a mutant allele, can also be called a mutant. The term 'mutation' is often used to describe the changed DNA as well as the process of changing.

It would be a mistake to think that every allele can be classed as either wild type or mutant. Eye colour in humans is variable, yet one does not describe a brown eyed person as normal and a blue eyed person as a mutant, although the allele for blue eyes probably arose by mutation of an allele for a darker eye colour. The existence of different alleles contributes to the normal range of variation found within a species.

2.2   *Phenotypic effects of mutant alleles*

The extent to which mutant alleles affect the phenotype is variable. Mutation is possible in any kind of tissue but a new mutant allele can be transmitted to the next generation only if it occurs in a cell which will ultimately give rise to gametes. **Somatic mutations** are those which occur in the body cells (**soma**) other than those destined for the production of gametes (the **germ line**). The somatic and germ line cells are differentiated very early in development. In a human female, the germ line cells reach prophase of meiosis before she is born.

Multiplication of body cells by mitosis is under the control of genes. If any of these genes should mutate, cells inheriting the mutant allele will divide in an uncontrolled manner and form an ever increasing mass of similar cells called a cancer. Such a mutation can occur in any kind of tissue. An example of a less injurious somatic mutation is one responsible for odd coloured eyes in humans. The genetic control of eye colour is complicated, but let us suppose that genotype *Bb* gives brown eyes and *bb* gives blue eyes. If, in a heterozygote, *B* mutates to *b* on one side of the developing foetus, then the eye which has cells containing *bb* will be blue and the other eye which develops from unmutated cells will be brown. Other tissues originating from the mutant cell will also carry the new mutant allele but its effects will be noticeable only in the eye. The trait of odd coloured eyes is not inherited because the gonads (ovaries and testes) are not affected by somatic mutation.

Mutant alleles arising in the germ line are capable of being transmitted to the next generation. However, the organism inheriting a newly mutated allele from one parent will normally inherit a different allele from the other. While the mutant allele may give rise to a non-functional gene product, the other allele by itself may be able to supply the cell's requirements. Thus the effect of the mutant allele will not be apparent in the phenotype; it is recessive. Recessivity and dominance are not properties of genes or traits but descriptions of the phenotypic consequences of interactions between two alleles.

Gene mutations or **point mutations** involve the addition or deletion of one or a few base pairs or the substitution of one base pair for another. Mutations involving larger segments of chromosomes, whole chromosomes or sets of chromosomes are called **chromosome mutations**. These do not necessarily generate new alleles but alter the number or rearrange the position of already existing ones. Chromosome mutations are discussed more fully in section 5.7. Figure 1 illustrates the consequences of some point mutations and shows that the gene product of an altered sequence of bases may be almost non-existent (allele 1), non-functional (allele 2), with impaired function (allele 3) or no different from the product of the original allele (allele 4).

Spontaneous mutation is a rare event. Estimates of mutation rate vary for different loci and different species. In humans about one in 10^5 gametes carries a new mutant allele at any particular gene locus. Considering that there are perhaps 50 000 gene loci, the probability that a gamete contains *any* new mutant allele is $50\,000 \times 10^{-5} = \frac{1}{2}$. The probability that a *zygote* will *not* contain a new mutant allele is therefore $\frac{1}{2} \times \frac{1}{2} = \frac{1}{4}$ (see section 2.6 for method). This means that about 75% of us carry at least one new mutant allele somewhere in our chromosomes. Remember that mutation at any specific gene locus is an extremely unlikely event so if you meet a genetics problem which you cannot immediately solve, think carefully before concluding that mutation is involved.

Figure 1 *Effects of different mutations on the product of a hypothetical gene*

Wild type allele   DNA strand   T A C C A A T G T G A C T A A A G G C T C G G G A C T
                   mRNA strand   A U G G U U A C A C U G A U U U C C G A G C C C U G A
                   Polypeptide   met   val   thr   leu   ile   ser   glu   pro STOP

Deletion of guanine
↓

Mutant allele 1   DNA strand   T A C C A A T T G A C T A A A G G C T C G G G A C T
                  mRNA strand   A U G G U U A A C U G A U U U C C G A G C C C U G A
                  Polypeptide   met   val   asn STOP

Deletion has given rise to the premature appearance of a terminator codon (UGA) so a polypeptide is produced which is very much shorter than normal.

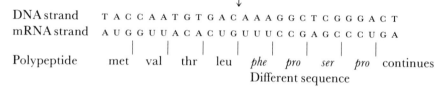

Deletion of thymine
↓

Mutant allele 2   DNA strand   T A C C A A T G T G A C A A A G G C T C G G G A C T
                  mRNA strand   A U G G U U A C A C U G U U U C C G A G C C C U G A

Polypeptide   met   val   thr   leu   *phe*   *pro*   *ser*   *pro*   continues

Different sequence

Deletion of a single base pair has caused the 'reading frame' to get out of step such that the wrong transfer RNAs are attracted to the mRNA strand and the wrong polypeptide is built. This is called a 'frameshift mutation'. Not only is a different sequence of amino acids incorporated but there is no longer a UGA terminator codon so the resulting polypeptide is longer than normal.

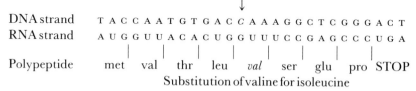

Substitution of cytosine for thymine
↓

Mutant allele 3   DNA strand   T A C C A A T G T G A C C A A A G G C T C G G G A C T
                  RNA strand   A U G G U U A C A C U G G U U U C C G A G C C C U G A

Polypeptide   met   val   thr   leu   *val*   ser   glu   pro   STOP

Substitution of valine for isoleucine

The substitution of a CG pair for a TA pair leads to a single amino acid substitution. The consequence for the function of the polypeptide may range from negligible to substantial depending on the significance of the amino acid that has been replaced. Sickle cell anaemia (see section 2.4) results from a single amino acid substitution in the haemoglobin molecule.

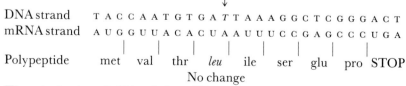

Substitution of thymine for cytosine
↓

Mutant allele 4   DNA strand   T A C C A A T G T G A T T A A A G G C T C G G G A C T
                  mRNA strand   A U G G U U A C A C U A A U U U C C G A G C C C U G A

Polypeptide   met   val   thr   *leu*   ile   ser   glu   pro   STOP

No change

The substitution of a TA pair for a CG pair makes no difference since both CUA and CUG code for leucine.

When describing the action of genes it is often necessary to make simple statements such as 'In *Drosophila*, *w* controls white eye colour and *W* controls red eye colour', a statement which suggests, erroneously, that there is a single gene locus which is responsible for eye colour. In reality, the products of a large number of genes interact in the development of every part of an animal or plant. We only recognize the existence of one of these genes when mutation occurs and gives rise to an altered phenotype (see also section 3.5). Conversely, one gene locus can affect more than one aspect of the phenotype ('character'). In *Drosophila*, *white* not only affects eye colour, but also behaviour and the pigmentation of internal organs. Albino mammals lack the enzyme tyrosinase which is involved in the conversion of tyrosine to melanin pigment. Lack of melanin is evident in hair, skin and eye colour and is also responsible for poor eyesight in albinos. Where a gene has more than one phenotypic effect, it is said to be **pleiotropic**. Another example of pleiotropy (or pleiotropism) is illustrated in Figure 2.

Figure 2 *Pleiotropic effects of the allele for cystic fibrosis in humans*

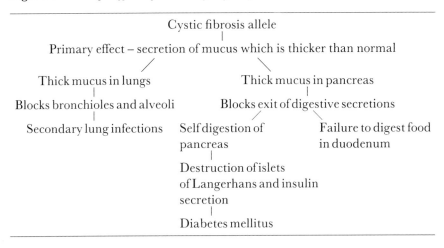

2.3 *Multiple alleles*

Over a period of time, an immense number of changes can occur anywhere in a gene, the coding region of which is, on average, about 1200–1500 base pairs. Each change gives rise to another allele so the number of possible alleles at a gene locus is also very large. When three or more alleles at a locus are known, the gene is said to have **multiple alleles**. In *Drosophila* for instance, a gene coding for a dehydrogenase enzyme has at least 32 alleles. Any individual fly, being diploid, can carry only two.

The ABO blood group system in humans is controlled by a series of multiple alleles. The blood group is determined by the type of protein present on the membrane of the red cells. Group A has only protein A, group B has protein B, group AB has both and group O has neither. Alleles of gene 'I', I^A and I^B, code for enzymes involved in the formation of proteins A and B respectively. A third allele, I^O, codes for no known enzyme. A person can have only two alleles, either both the same or two different ones so there are six possible genotypes which are shown in Table 1. These genotypes correspond to only four phenotypes because two have only the A protein and two have only the B protein.

Table 1 *Blood group genotypes and phenotypes*

Genotype	Phenotype
$I^A I^A$	Group A
$I^A I^O$	Group A
$I^A I^B$	Group AB
$I^B I^B$	Group B
$I^B I^O$	Group B
$I^O I^O$	Group O

In many texts, the alleles I^A, I^B and I^O are called simply A, B and O. This practice can lead to confusion for two reasons; the distinction between genotype and phenotype is not made clear and it obscures the fact that all three are alleles at the same locus.

A multiple allele system determines coat colour in the rabbit. The wild type coat colour is called agouti and each hair has a grey base, a yellow band and a black tip. Albino is the condition where there is no pigment at all so the fur is white. When homozygous agouti and albino rabbits are crossed, the F_1 progeny are all agouti and the F_2 progeny show a ratio of 3 agouti:1 albino. This demonstrates that agouti and albino are controlled by a pair of alleles with agouti being dominant. Chinchilla rabbits are silvery grey because they lack the yellow band in each hair. When chinchilla and agouti homozygotes are crossed, all the F_1 progeny are agouti and the F_2 progeny appear in the ratio 3 agouti:1 chinchilla. Again these results show that there is a pair of alleles controlling coat colour with agouti being dominant to chinchilla. If *agouti* is allelic to (at the same gene locus as) *chinchilla* and *albino*, then there must be three alleles at this locus and the symbols are C, c^{ch} and c respectively. Another colour pattern is controlled by a fourth allele, *himalayan* (c^h). Himalayan rabbits are white except for black feet, ears, nose and tail. Crosses amongst animals of the various coat colours reveals that agouti is dominant to all, albino is recessive to all and chinchilla is dominant to himalayan. Figure 3 shows the inheritance of agouti, himalayan and albino.

Figure 3 *Two crosses demonstrating multiple allelism in the rabbit*

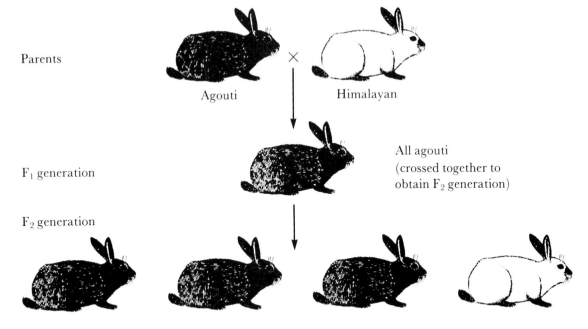

Parents

Agouti   ×   Himalayan

F₁ generation

All agouti
(crossed together to
obtain F₂ generation)

F₂ generation

Ratio of 3 agouti : 1 himalayan

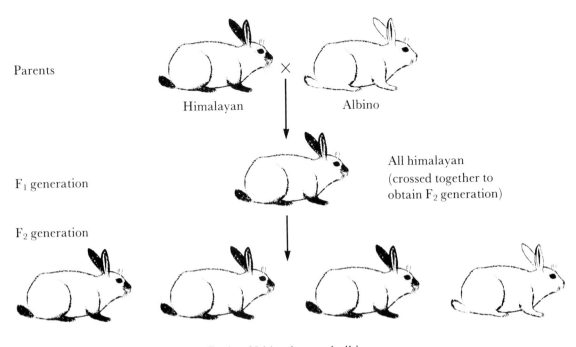

Parents

Himalayan   ×   Albino

F₁ generation

All himalayan
(crossed together to
obtain F₂ generation)

F₂ generation

Ratio of 3 himalayan : 1 albino

2.3.1   What are the phenotypes corresponding to the following genotypes?
(i) $c^{ch}c^h$ (ii) Cc^h (iii) c^hc

2.3.2   How many different genotypes correspond to each of the following phenotypes?
(i) agouti   (ii) albino   (iii) himalayan

2.3.3   When carrying out organ transplants, it is important to match the tissue types of the donor and recipient. Tissue types are genetically determined and one of the loci has 8 alleles. How many possible genotypes are there at this locus?

2.4   *Incomplete dominance and codominance*

The characters which Mendel investigated showed **complete dominance**, which means that the heterozygote has the same phenotype as the homozygous dominant. The two cannot normally be distinguished except by breeding experiments (see section 1.4). In many cases of monohybrid inheritance, this is not so. Neither allele is dominant to the other and the heterozygote can be recognized phenotypically.

It is conventional to use a capital letter for the dominant allele and a small letter for the recessive one but where there is no dominance, the alleles must be represented differently. In *Antirrhinum* (snapdragon) a gene locus for flower colour has two alleles, neither dominant. Let us call them a^1 and a^2. The genotype a^1a^1 has red flowers, a^2a^2 has white flowers and the heterozygote a^1a^2 is pink. Table 2 shows the expected F_2 ratio.

It seems at first sight that the red and white traits blend in the F_1 generation to give an intermediate colour. This apparent 'blending inheritance' is often observed but the fact that red and white flowers appear again in the F_2 generation is proof that the alleles themselves do not blend. They remain as separate units when they are together in the F_1 plants. They are free to segregate at gamete formation and recombine at fertilization to give a typical Mendelian ratio.

Flower colour in *Antirrhinum* shows partial or **incomplete dominance** because the phenotype of the heterozygote is intermediate between that of both homozygotes. The allele a^1 might be supposed to produce an enzyme necessary for the development of red pigment while the a^2 allele does not. a^1a^1 homozygotes produce sufficient enzyme for the petals to develop the full red colour. In heterozygotes, only the a^1 allele produces the enzyme. Consequently there is a smaller amount and the petals are pink. In the a^2a^2 homozygote, neither allele is producing the enzyme and the petals remain uncoloured, i.e. white.

The degree of dominance may be difficult to determine because it depends very much on the level of observation of the phenotype. Mendel discovered that in the seed shape character, smooth is dominant to

Table 2 *A monohybrid cross in* Antirrhinum *involving incomplete dominance*

Parental genotype	a^1a^1	a^2a^2
Parental phenotype	Red	White
Parental gametes	All a^1	All a^2

Cross fertilization
↓

F$_1$ genotype a^1a^2

F$_1$ phenotype   Pink

F$_1$ gametes $\frac{1}{2}a^1$ and $\frac{1}{2}a^2$

F$_2$ genotypes
shown in the table   Gametes from male

		$\frac{1}{2}a^1$	$\frac{1}{2}a^2$
Gametes from female	$\frac{1}{2}a^1$	$\frac{1}{4}a^1a^1$	$\frac{1}{4}a^1a^2$
	$\frac{1}{2}a^2$	$\frac{1}{4}a^1a^2$	$\frac{1}{4}a^2a^2$

F$_2$ genotypic ratio $1\,a^1a^1 : 2\,a^1a^2 : 1\,a^2a^2$
F$_2$ phenotypic ratio   1 red : 2 pink : 1 white

wrinkled. Smooth homozygotes and heterozygotes cannot be distinguished by looking at them with the naked eye. However, they are distinguishable at the microscopic level. Cotyledons from smooth homozygotes are packed with starch grains while wrinkled seeds contain very few. Heterozygotes have an intermediate number. Starch adsorbs water, so cotyledons containing it are plump and rounded while those with sugar rather than starch hold less water and so appear wrinkled. Heterozygotes have enough starch to fill out their cotyledons to the same extent as the smooth homozygotes. Thus, at the microscopic level, smooth is incompletely dominant to wrinkled, but at the macroscopic level, dominance appears to be complete.

Codominance is similar to but not quite the same as incomplete dominance. Again the heterozygote is phenotypically distinguishable from both homozygotes but codominant alleles both make a contribution so that the phenotype of the heterozygote shows features of both traits. Like incomplete dominance, codominance gives an expected **1:2:1** phenotypic ratio in an F$_2$ generation.

In humans, there is a mutant allele of the gene which codes for the β-globin chain in haemoglobin. A single base pair substitution has produced an allele which codes for the amino acid valine instead of glutamic acid in the sixth position of the chain. The mutant allele is known as Hb^S and the normal allele is Hb^A. The haemoglobin of the homozygote Hb^S/Hb^S is abnormal. When deoxygenated, its solubility is low and it precipitates in the form of angular crystals. These distort the red cell into a crescent or sickle shape in which state it is susceptible to mechanical damage. Many cells are destroyed and the person suffers from the painful and often fatal disease of **sickle cell anaemia**. In the heterozygote, at least half of the haemoglobin is normal and the cells do not have the same tendency to distort in the tissues. The heterozygote suffers little if at all from anaemia. However, if the red cells are viewed under the microscope at a low oxygen concentration, some will become sickle shaped so the heterozygote is said to show **sickle cell trait**. Hb^S and Hb^A are considered to be codominant because they both make a contribution to the haemoglobin of the heterozygote who can be identified by observation of the red blood cells. However, if we take anaemia as the phenotype, then Hb^S would be regarded as recessive. In fact with any gene, the nearer one gets to the gene product, the less meaningful is the concept of dominance.

2.4.1   How would you describe the dominance relationships between alleles I^A, I^B and I^O which were introduced in section 2.3?

2.5   *Lethal alleles*

There are certain gene loci whose gene product is essential for life. Any allele which fails to produce it will be **lethal** in the homozygous state, and the phenotype of the heterozygote may also be affected. In the fruit fly *Drosophila* the dominant allele Cy causes curly wings when heterozygous (Cy/cy) but is lethal when homozygous. Cy/Cy homozygotes do not survive to the adult stage. Flies homozygous for the recessive, wild type allele (cy/cy) have normal, straight wings. The phenotypes are illustrated in Figure 4. (Note that where more than one letter is used to denote a

Figure 4 *The fruit fly,* Drosophila melanogaster

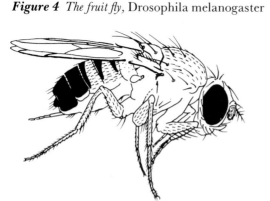

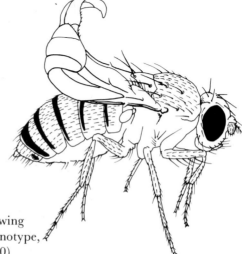

(a) Wild type male (×20)

(b) Female showing the mutant phenotype, curly wing (×20)

single allele, a bar, /, may be used between the allele symbols. It may also be used where alleles are represented by a single letter. Thus B/b means the same as Bb.)

Genes which are lethal when homozygous but not when heterozygous are called **recessive lethal** genes. This example also serves to illustrate the point made in section 2.2 that dominance and recessivity are not properties of the alleles themselves but describe their relationship to other alleles at the same gene locus. The allele Cy is dominant with respect to its effects on wing shape but recessive in its effects on viability. Recessive lethal genes bring about a modification of the expected $3:1$ phenotypic ratio in the progeny of two heterozygotes (Table 3). The expected genotypic ratio in Table 3 is 1 Cy/Cy : 2 Cy/cy : 1 cy/cy but Cy/Cy does not survive to the adult stage and the observed ratio is 2 curly (Cy/cy) : 1 normal (cy/cy). Such a $2:1$ ratio is typical where the allele with a dominant visible effect is lethal in the homozygous condition.

Table 3 *Outcome of a cross between curly winged* Drosophila

Parental genotype	Cy/cy			Cy/cy
Parental phenotype	Curly			Curly
Parental gametes	$\frac{1}{2}Cy$ and $\frac{1}{2}cy$			$\frac{1}{2}Cy$ and $\frac{1}{2}cy$

Genotypes of progeny shown in the table			Gametes from male	
			$\frac{1}{2}Cy$	$\frac{1}{2}cy$
Gametes from female	$\frac{1}{2}Cy$		$\frac{1}{4}Cy/Cy$	$\frac{1}{4}Cy/cy$
	$\frac{1}{2}cy$		$\frac{1}{4}Cy/cy$	$\frac{1}{4}cy/cy$

Observed phenotypic ratio in progeny   2 curly (Cy/cy) : 1 wild type (cy/cy)

2.6 *Mendelian ratios and probability*

The Mendelian ratios, $3:1$, $1:2:1$, $1:1$, $2:1$ and others to be described, are expected ratios when large numbers of progeny are available for counting. The progeny will not always occur in these ratios and the smaller the family, the less likely that the offspring will fit the expected ratio exactly. In humans for instance, the sex ratio is approximately $1:1$ but this does not mean that every family has equal numbers of boys and girls. It means that every time fertilization occurs, there is an equal chance that the zygote is male or female. Even where parents have several boys but no girl, the chance that the next child will be a girl remains unchanged.

If there are four rabbits in the litter of a cross between two animals heterozygous for albinism, there are not necessarily going to be three coloured and one albino. Each rabbit in the litter has a 1 in 4 chance of being albino. Just by chance, the whole litter could be albino. For a practical demonstration, take two coins to represent the heterozygous parents. Toss both coins four times and note how many times you get two heads, two tails or one of each, representing offspring genotypes of *AA*, *aa* and *Aa* respectively. The more times you toss the coins, the more likely it is that you will get a ratio of 1 both heads : 2 one of each : 1 both tails.

Mendelian ratios are used to estimate the *probability* that certain phenotypes and genotypes will occur. Probabilities can be expressed as fractions, proportions or percentages. For example, the probability that a child will be a girl is $\frac{1}{2}$ or 0·5 or 50%. It is less confusing if you keep to one method; fractions are used in this section.

How did we calculate the probability that a child will be a girl? We know that it can only be one of two sexes. 'One out of two' is expressed $\frac{1}{2}$. When calculating the probability of certain genotypes or phenotypes occurring in the progeny of a cross, it is often helpful to draw a Punnett square. The number of boxes in the square gives the number of possible outcomes which is the denominator (the number below the line) in the fraction. The Punnett square in Table 4 shows that there are four possible combinations of gametes in the cross *Aa* × *Aa*. The probability of genotype *aa* in the progeny is one out of four, i.e. $\frac{1}{4}$. The probability of genotype *Aa* in the progeny is $\frac{2}{4}$ or $\frac{1}{2}$ because there are two ways that this combination can come about. These probabilities can be stated more simply thus, P(*aa*) = $\frac{1}{4}$, P(*Aa*) = $\frac{1}{2}$. Similarly, P(coloured) = $\frac{3}{4}$.

Table 4 *Punnett square giving the expected outcome of a cross between two rabbits heterozygous for albinism (genotype Aa)*

	Gametes from male	
	$\frac{1}{2} A$	$\frac{1}{2} a$
$\frac{1}{2} A$	$\frac{1}{4} AA$	$\frac{1}{4} Aa$
$\frac{1}{2} a$	$\frac{1}{4} Aa$	$\frac{1}{4} aa$

Gametes from female

Table 4 gives the probability of occurrence of each type of gamete and it can be seen that the zygote probabilities can also be calculated by multiplying together the probabilities of the gametes involved in their formation.

It is important to realize that each fertilization event is quite independent. Every rabbit in the litter in our example has a $\frac{1}{4}$ chance of being *aa* at conception, regardless of the genotypes of its litter mates. If there were only two rabbits in the litter, the probability that both of them will be albino is calculated by multiplying together the probabilities of each of them being albino.

$$P(\text{1st rabbit is albino}) = \tfrac{1}{4}$$
$$P(\text{2nd rabbit is albino}) = \tfrac{1}{4}$$
$$P(\text{both are albino}) = \tfrac{1}{4} \times \tfrac{1}{4} = \tfrac{1}{16}$$

2.6.1　Two rabbits heterozygous for albinism were crossed. What is the probability that the first rabbit in the litter is a coloured male?

2.6.2　What is the probability that the two offspring in the above litter are both albino females? (First find the probability that each of them is both albino and female.)

2.6.3　One person in 25 is heterozygous for cystic fibrosis (see section 2.2). What is the probability that a married couple are both heterozygous for cystic fibrosis?

2.7 *Pedigrees*

A **pedigree** is a record of the ancestry of an individual. Strictly speaking, a 'pedigree animal' is one for which there exists a record of its ancestors, although the phrase is generally restricted to an animal whose ancestors are all of a similar kind, e.g. the same breed of dog. A pedigree in the form of a chart can be used to illustrate the transmission of a heritable condition in a family. The symbols used are shown in Figure 5.

Figure 5 *Symbols used in a pedigree chart*

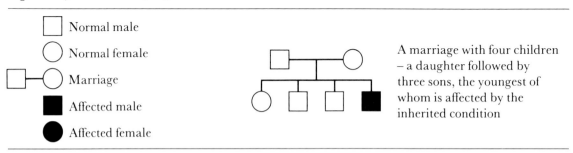

2.7.1　Study the pedigree in Figure 6 opposite.
 (i) Who is affected by the hereditary condition?
 (ii) Who is Daniel's wife?
 (iii) Who is Ivy's sister?
 (iv) Who is Gail's cousin?
 (v) Who are John's grandparents?
 (vi) Who is Henry's uncle?

Figure 6 *Example of a pedigree*

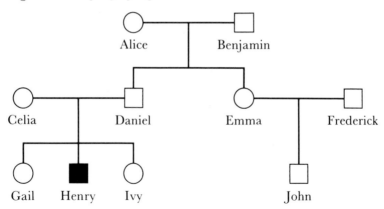

2.8 Summary

All new alleles arise from pre-existing ones by the process of mutation and although mutation of any particular locus is a rare event, there is so much DNA in a cell that newly mutated alleles are not uncommon. New mutant alleles may arise in somatic tissue and will not be inherited. Those which arise in the germ line can be inherited but do not necessarily have a noticeable effect on the phenotype. The gene product of a new mutant allele is not necessarily very much affected by the mutation but in some cases the gene product is missing altogether. If the product is essential for life, a gene which fails to produce it will be lethal in the homozygous state.

Although Mendel recognized only two alternative 'factors' for each character, we now know that potentially hundreds of alleles can exist at each gene locus. However, a diploid organism can carry only two, so multiple alleles still conform to Mendel's Law of Segregation.

Dominance and recessivity are not properties of the alleles themselves but describe the relationships between alleles at a locus. At the level of the gene product, there is no such thing as dominance but the product of one allele may have more noticeable effects than the other on the organism's appearance, physiology or behaviour, all aspects of the phenotype. Only if there is no detectable difference between a homozygote and a heterozygote can an allele be described as completely dominant. Many alleles show varying degrees of dominance.

Mendelian ratios enable us to calculate the probability of certain genotypes and phenotypes occurring in the progeny of a cross. The new ratios introduced in this chapter are:

$1:2:1$ phenotypic and genotypic ratio from the cross $a^1a^2 \times a^1a^2$ where

a^1 and a^2 are incompletely dominant or codominant. The genotypic ratio is $1\ a^1a^1:2\ a^1a^2:1\ a^2a^2$

$2:1$ phenotypic and genotypic ratio from $Aa \times Aa$ where A is lethal when homozygous. The ratio is $(1\ AA$ – dies$):2\ Aa$ (dominant trait)$:1\ aa$ (recessive trait).

Key words

	Section		Section
chromosome mutation	2.2	pedigree	2.7
codominance	2.4	pleiotropic	2.2
complete dominance	2.4	point mutation	2.2
gene mutation	2.2	recessive lethal allele	2.5
germ line	2.2	sickle cell anaemia	2.4
incomplete dominance	2.4	sickle cell trait	2.4
lethal allele	2.5	soma	2.2
multiple alleles	2.3	somatic mutation	2.2
mutant allele	2.1	wild type	2.1
mutation	2.1		

Answers

2.3.1 (i) Chinchilla; (ii) agouti; (iii) himalayan.

2.3.2 (i) Four, C/C, C/c^{ch}, C/c^h, C/c; (ii) one, c/c; (iii) two, c^h/c^h, c^h/c. (A bar, /, is used between allele symbols for greater clarity. See section 2.5.)

2.3.3 Thirty-six. Each person has two alleles in any combination. The number of possible combinations can be shown in a table. Each different combination is marked by an asterisk.

alleles	1	2	3	4	5	6	7	8
1	*	*	*	*	*	*	*	*
2		*	*	*	*	*	*	*
3			*	*	*	*	*	*
4				*	*	*	*	*
5					*	*	*	*
6						*	*	*
7							*	*
8								*

The number of possible combinations of two alleles taken from n alleles can also be calculated from the formula $\frac{1}{2}n(n+1)$.

Another gene locus which determines tissue type has 40 alleles, giving 820 possible genotypes at this locus. There are millions of different tissue types, meaning that it is almost impossible to match exactly donor with recipient. The more closely related two people are, the more likely they are to have alleles in common.

2.4.1 I^A and I^B are codominant because the heterozygote I^A/I^B has both proteins. I^O is recessive to both because I^A/I^O and I^B/I^O are phenotypically indistinguishable from I^A/I^A and I^B/I^B respectively. Allele I^O could be called i.

2.6.1   P(coloured) $= \frac{3}{4}$,   P(male) $= \frac{1}{2}$,   P(coloured male) $= \frac{3}{4} \times \frac{1}{2} = \frac{3}{8}$.

2.6.2   P(albino) $= \frac{1}{4}$,   P(female) $= \frac{1}{2}$,   P(albino female) $= \frac{1}{4} \times \frac{1}{2} = \frac{1}{8}$, P(both offspring are albino females) $= \frac{1}{8} \times \frac{1}{8} = \frac{1}{64}$.

2.6.3 $\frac{1}{25} \times \frac{1}{25} = \frac{1}{625}$.

2.7.1   (i) Henry;   (ii) Celia;   (iii) Gail;   (iv) John;   (v) Alice and Benjamin; (vi) Frederick.

Problems

13   Red Poll cattle are chestnut red. When crossed to White Shorthorn, the calves have a mixture of red and white hairs, giving an overall colouring called roan. Give the possible phenotypes of the offspring of the following crosses and the probability with which they will occur.
(a) roan × roan,   (b) roan × white,   (c) roan × red.

14   A man and a woman, both able to roll their tongues, had four children. Two children were able to roll their tongues and two were not. Using suitable symbols, give the genotypes of the parents and the children.

15   Thalassaemia is a serious form of anaemia which is genetically determined. Mario and Carmen are a normal, healthy couple who have just married. Their parents are also normal but both Mario and Carmen had sisters who died in childhood from thalassaemia.
(a) Is thalassaemia dominant or recessive?
(b) Carmen does not have the disease, but what is the probability that she is a carrier (heterozygous)? (Hint: use a Punnett square.)
(c) If Mario and Carmen have a child, what is the probability that it will have thalassaemia?

16   A budgerigar fancier bred together homozygous Mauve (dark blue) with homozygous Skyblue (pale blue) birds and obtained all Cobalt (mid blue) progeny. In an attempt to breed more Cobalts he bred together the F_1 progeny. To his surprise, he obtained some Mauves and Skyblues as well as Cobalts. What proportions of the three different phenotypes would he get?

17 The colour of wild mice is agouti while mice lacking the black band in each hair are yellow. In 1905 a geneticist reported that he had been unable to get homozygous yellow mice. A number of geneticists then pooled their data on the results of crosses between yellow mice and found that out of a total of 1598 progeny, 1063 were yellow and 535 were non-yellow. Individual litters tended to be smaller than normal.

(a) What is the approximate ratio of yellow : non-yellow in the progeny?

(b) What would be the best way to test whether a yellow mouse is homozygous or heterozygous?

(c) As far as body colour is concerned, which is the dominant allele?

(d) As far as viability is concerned, which is the dominant allele?

18 Some poppies have a purple spot at the base of each petal while others do not. Certain crosses were made between different poppy plants and their progeny were collected. The results are shown below.

Parents	Progeny
Spotted no. 1 × spotted no. 2	137 spotted
Unspotted no. 1 × unspotted no. 2	128 unspotted
Spotted no. 1 × spotted no. 3	87 spotted and 30 unspotted
Spotted no. 3 × unspotted no. 3	66 spotted and 52 unspotted

Using suitable symbols, give the genotypes of the three spotted and three unspotted plants.

19 A cat fancier bought two Tonkinese cats. These are characterized by a pale brown coat with darker legs, tail, nose and ears (the points). She mated the cats together and obtained a litter of two. One kitten was Siamese (pale cream body and dark points) and the other was a Burmese (dark brown body with darker points). The three phenotypes are under the control of a single gene locus.

(a) Using suitable symbols, give the genotypes of Tonkinese, Siamese and Burmese.

(b) What phenotypes should the breeder cross in order to get litters of
(i) all Siamese,   (i) all Burmese,   (iii) all Tonkinese?

20 Ichthyosis in mice is a condition where the skin is dry, hard and scaly with little hair. The table shows the results of mating experiments.

Parents	Progeny		
	Normal	Ichthyotic	Total
Homozygous normal × homozygous ichthyotic	54	0	54
Heterozygote × heterozygote	529	99	628
Heterozygote × homozygous ichthyotic	9	3	12

    (a) Is ichthyosis dominant or recessive? Give a reason for your answer.

    (b) What are the ratios of normal to ichthyotic in the second and third crosses?

    (c) How can you account for these ratios?

21   Katherine is blood group A, like her mother. Her elder sister is group B and her brother is group O. What are the genotypes of their parents?

22   The background colour of the shell of the snail *Cepaea nemoralis* may be brown, pink or yellow. The colour is controlled by a single gene locus with three alleles. c^B codes for brown and is dominant to c^P which codes for pink. c^Y codes for yellow and is recessive to both of the other alleles. What will be the expected phenotypic ratios in the offspring of the following crosses?

    (a) homozygous brown × yellow;   (b) $c^B c^P$ × yellow;

    (c) $c^B c^P$ × $c^B c^P$;   (d) $c^P c^Y$ × yellow;   (e) $c^B c^Y$ × $c^P c^Y$.

23   In budgerigars, the colour of the wings is controlled by a multiple allele series. The normal full colour (symbol C) is dominant to all the others. Greywing (c^g) is dominant to clearwing (c^w) and dilute (c^d). Clearwing is dominant to dilute. A breeder had a clearwing bird and paired it with a full colour mate. The progeny included full colour, clearwing and dilute. The dilute progeny were particularly attractive so she bred the parents again.

    (a) If they produce only one chick, what is the probability that it is dilute?

    (b) If they produce two chicks, what is the probability that they will both be full colour?

24   Charles Darwin observed that the seeds of peaches may grow into trees bearing nectarines and the seeds of nectarines may grow into trees bearing peaches. Assume that the difference in phenotype is controlled by two alleles at a single gene locus.

    (a) Explain Darwin's observations.

    (b) What experiments could be done to discover whether peach or nectarine is the dominant phenotype?

25   A beautiful blonde, let's call her Miss X, gave birth to an equally beautiful blonde daughter. Miss X was not sure which of her two boyfriends, Y or Z, was the father. Y was blonde but Z had brown hair, so Miss X thought that Y must be the father and told him he must help to support the child. Now Y had studied A-level biology at school and knew something about the inheritance of blood groups. He knew that his is quite rare, AB, and he arranged for Miss X, the baby and Z to have blood tests. The results were as follows.

        Miss X, group A.   The baby, group O.   Z, group B.

Z said: 'The baby can't be mine because she's got a different blood group.'

Miss X said: 'Well, she's certainly mine, but how come she's got a different blood group from me?'

'Dada?' queried the baby.

Y breathed a sigh of relief and explained to the father and mother how the baby inherited its blood group from both of them. What did he tell them?

3 Dihybrid inheritance

3.1 Mendel's experiments and conclusions

In his first experiments, Mendel investigated the inheritance of variation in only one character. In his second set of experiments, he crossed pea plants differing simultaneously in two characters in order to find out whether or not the characters had any influence on each other's inheritance. A cross in which two loci are considered is called a **dihybrid cross**.

One of Mendel's experiments concerned two seed characters, shape and colour of cotyledons. He crossed pure breeding plants grown from smooth, yellow seeds with pure breeding plants grown from wrinkled, green seeds. The F_1 and F_2 progeny are shown in Table 1. Notice that all the seeds are either yellow or green *and* either smooth or wrinkled.

Table 1 *The results of a breeding experiment with two seed characters*

Parental generation phenotype			Smooth, yellow × wrinkled, green			
F_1 generation phenotype			All smooth and yellow (allowed to self fertilize to obtain F_2)			
F_2 generation phenotype			Seed colour			
			Yellow	Green	Total	Ratio
	Seed shape	Smooth	315	108	423	3·18
		Wrinkled	101	32	133	:1
		Total	416	140	556	
		Ratio	2·97	: 1		

All dihybrid crosses can be treated as two separate monohybrid crosses. In the seed shape character, the F_2 seeds approximate to the theoretical ratio of 3 smooth : 1 wrinkled, and for the seed colour character, the ratio is approximately 3 yellow : 1 green. If shape is inherited independently of colour, it is possible to predict the proportion of the F_2 seeds which are both smooth and yellow by the method explained in section 2.6.

3.1.1 (a) In an F_2 generation such as that shown in Table 1, what is the probability that a seed is smooth (P(smooth))?
  (b) What is P(yellow)?
  (c) What is P(smooth and yellow)?
  (d) What fraction of the 556 progeny is expected to be smooth and yellow?
  (e) How many of the 556 progeny are expected to be smooth and yellow?
  (f) Is the expected number similar to the actual number obtained in Table 1?

If you calculate the probabilities of the other three combinations of traits in a similar manner, you will find that the phenotypic classes occur in the proportions shown in Table 2. These proportions are expected only if shape and colour are inherited independently of each other.

Table 2 *Expected proportions of phenotypes in the F_2 generation*

Smooth and yellow	$\frac{9}{16}$
Smooth and green	$\frac{3}{16}$
Wrinkled and yellow	$\frac{3}{16}$
Wrinkled and green	$\frac{1}{16}$

3.1.2 Using the information in Table 2, calculate the number of the 556 F_2 progeny which are expected to be
  (a) smooth and green,   (b) wrinkled and yellow,
  (c) wrinkled and green.

The numbers which Mendel observed in the results of his dihybrid cross agree with the numbers that are expected if the inheritance of seed shape has no effect on the inheritance of colour and vice versa. So he was able to formulate what has become known as his **second law**. In modern terms, this states that the segregation of one pair of alleles is independent of the segregation of a second pair and that any combination of alleles can occur in the zygotes. It is also called the **Law of Independent Assortment**. Because the alleles at one gene locus segregate at random with respect to alleles at another gene locus, the expected phenotypic ratio in the F_2 progeny of a dihybrid cross is **9:3:3:1** being

9 (both dominant traits)
3 (1 dominant and 1 recessive trait)
3 (1 recessive and 1 dominant trait)
1 (both recessive traits)

We have seen how the phenotypic ratio can be calculated by the probability method. The genotypic ratio can be calculated in the same way but a more visual approach using a Punnett square is often more helpful. Table 3 shows the same cross as in Table 2 with genotypes added. Notice that a gamete has both an allele for colour and an allele for shape. There are four kinds of gametes from both F_1 males and F_1 females, giving rise to sixteen combinations in the F_2 generation.

Table 3 *A dihybrid cross showing the use of a Punnett square*

Parental generation:			
Phenotype	Smooth, yellow	×	wrinkled, green
Genotype	*SS YY*		*ss yy*
Gametes	*S Y*		*s y*
F_1 generation:			
Phenotype		Smooth, yellow	
Genotype		*Ss Yy*	

F_2 generation genotypes are shown in the table — Gametes from F_1 female

Gametes from F_1 male	Shape	Colour	$\frac{1}{2}S$		$\frac{1}{2}s$		Shape locus 'S'
			$\frac{1}{2}Y$	$\frac{1}{2}y$	$\frac{1}{2}Y$	$\frac{1}{2}y$	Colour locus 'Y'
	$\frac{1}{2}S$	$\frac{1}{2}Y$	*SS YY*	*SS Yy*	*Ss YY*	*Ss Yy*	
		$\frac{1}{2}y$	*SS Yy*	*SS yy*	*Ss Yy*	*Ss yy*	
	$\frac{1}{2}s$	$\frac{1}{2}Y$	*Ss YY*	*Ss Yy*	*ss YY*	*ss Yy*	
		$\frac{1}{2}y$	*Ss Yy*	*Ss yy*	*ss Yy*	*ss yy*	

3.1.3 (a) Copy out the Punnett square in Table 3. Decide which phenotype corresponds to each of the genotypes and use four different colours to shade in the boxes appropriately.
(b) What phenotypic ratio does your Punnett square show?

3.1.4 A plant with the genotype *Aa Bb* is selfed. In the progeny
(a) what is P(*AA*); (b) what is P(*Bb*); (c) what is P(*AA Bb*)?
(d) *AA Bb* corresponds to *SS Yy* in the Punnett square in Table 3. How many of the combinations are *SS Yy*? Does this agree with your calculation in part (c)?

3.2 The dihybrid testcross

The genotypes *SS YY*, *Ss YY*, *SS Yy* and *Ss Yy* all have the same phenotype, smooth and yellow. In order to discover the genotype of a plant grown from a smooth, yellow seed, a testcross can be done in just the same way as for a monohybrid cross. A testcross is always made to a homozygous recessive and in the case of a dihybrid cross, to the **double homozygous recessive**. In the example we are using, the double homozygous recessive is *ss yy* (wrinkled and green). The outcome of one such cross is shown in Table 4.

Table 4 *The outcome of a cross between Ss Yy and ss yy*

		Gametes from smooth, yellow parent			
		$\frac{1}{4}SY$	$\frac{1}{4}Sy$	$\frac{1}{4}sY$	$\frac{1}{4}sy$
Gametes from wrinkled, green parent	All *s y*	$\frac{1}{4}Ss\,Yy$	$\frac{1}{4}Ss\,yy$	$\frac{1}{4}ss\,Yy$	$\frac{1}{4}ss\,yy$
	Phenotype	Smooth, yellow	Smooth, green	Wrinkled, yellow	Wrinkled, green

Table 4 shows the dihybrid testcross (or backcross) genotypic and phenotypic ratio of **1 : 1 : 1 : 1** which is obtained when a double heterozygote is crossed to a double homozygous recessive.

3.2.1 What would be the genotypes of the progeny from the following crosses and in what proportions would they be expected?
(a) *AA Bb* × *aa bb*;   (b) *Tt zz* × *tt zz*;   (c) *Gg Hh* × *gg hh*.

3.3 *The physical basis of the Law of Independent Assortment*

We saw in section 1.5 that a pair of alleles segregates at gamete formation when homologous chromosomes move apart during anaphase I of meiosis. A cell has several pairs of homologous chromosomes behaving in this way. Table 5 shows the chromosome numbers for several animal and plant species.

Table 5 *Some chromosome numbers*

Common name	Scientific name	Number of homologous pairs of chromosomes
Tomato	*Lycopersicon esculentum*	12
Garden pea	*Pisum sativum*	7
White clover	*Trifolium repens*	16
Maize	*Zea mays*	10
Fruit fly	*Drosophila melanogaster*	4
Horse	*Equus caballus*	32
Human	*Homo sapiens*	23
Mouse	*Mus musculus*	20
Chimpanzee	*Pan troglodytes*	24

Figure 1 *Segregation of alleles A and a, and alleles B and b in a double heterozygote Aa Bb*

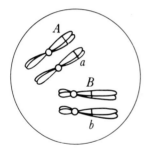

(i) At prophase I of meiosis, the two homologues of each pair come to lie side by side (chiasmata have been omitted).

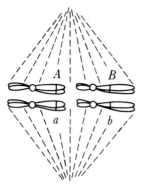

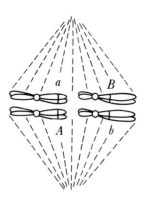

(ii) At metaphase I, the two pairs of homologues become attached to the spindle equator. The two possible orientations are shown.

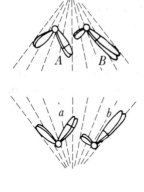

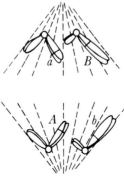

(iii) At anaphase I, the homologues separate. *A* can go to the same pole as *B* (and *a* with *b*) as shown at the left. Or *a* and *B* can go together (and *A* with *b*) as shown at the right.

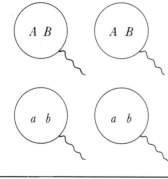

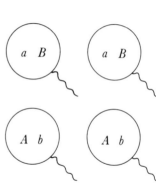

(iv) After the second meiotic division, the four gametes may have the allele combinations shown either at the left or at the right (but see section 5.2).

At meiosis anaphase I, the members of all the homologous pairs move apart. All the maternal homologues separate from the paternal ones and the two kinds move in opposite directions, but either kind can move to either pole of the spindle. The consequence is that the two nuclei resulting from the first meiotic division each contain one complete set of chromosomes being made up of one homologue, either maternal or paternal, from each pair. In human cells, containing 23 pairs of chromosomes, the number of different combinations of maternal and paternal homologues in products of the first meiotic division is 2^{23}, or more than eight million! (See, however, section 5.2.)

In dihybrid crosses we are interested in only two pairs of homologues. Mendel found that two pairs of alleles segregated independently because the characters he used were controlled by loci on two different pairs of homologues. It must be stressed that Mendel himself knew nothing of chromosomes and genes but was led to his conclusions by the ratios of the different combinations of traits in the progeny of his experimental crosses. Independent assortment means that the segregation of one pair of alleles is unaffected by the segregation of another pair and four different types of gametes are produced in equal numbers. Figure 1 shows diagrammatically the segregation of two pairs of alleles in a double heterozygote *Aa Bb*.

Figure 1 represents meiosis in a male where millions of gametes are being produced. A large number of cells are undergoing meiosis at the same time so on average, $\frac{1}{4}$ of the gametes will be *A B*, $\frac{1}{4}$ *a b*, $\frac{1}{4}$ *A b* and $\frac{1}{4}$ *a B*. A female mammal produces relatively few gametes but again, in a double heterozygote, each gamete will carry one of four possible combinations of genes. Thus both sexes produce four kinds of gametes in equal proportions and any kind of female gamete can be fertilized by any kind of male gamete so at fertilization, there are $4 \times 4 = 16$ possible combinations of gametes. Because of dominance relationships, these 16 genotypes fall into the phenotypic ratio of $9:3:3:1$.

3.4 *Interaction between genes at different loci*

Two alleles at a single locus always affect the same character, and the way that the alleles interact with each other is described by the terms dominant, recessive, incompletely dominant and codominant (see sections 1.1 and 2.4). In the dihybrid cross example explored in sections 3.1 and 3.2, each of the two gene loci controls a different character. However, it is not unusual for a single character to be under the influence of two (or more) gene loci.

One of the earliest known examples of such a character is the shape of the comb in the domestic fowl. Two gene loci are known which affect comb shape, 'P' and 'R'. There are two alleles at each locus which segregate independently according to Mendel's second law. The effect on comb shape of alleles at the 'P' locus depends on what alleles are present at the 'R' locus in the same bird. Four comb shapes can be recognized and they are illustrated in Figure 2.

Figure 2 *Comb shapes in domestic fowl*

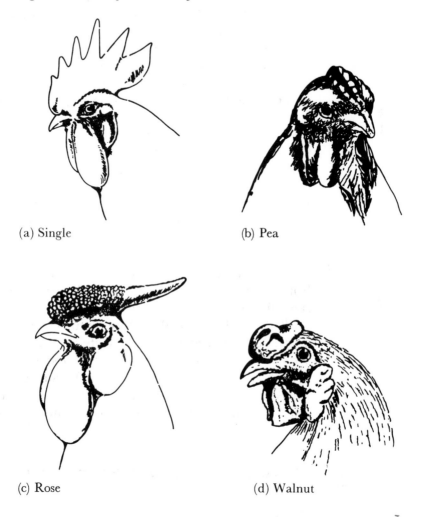

(a) Single

(b) Pea

(c) Rose

(d) Walnut

If a rose combed breed (e.g. Hamburgh) is crossed with a pea combed breed (e.g. Brahma), the comb of the F_1 birds is described as walnut. At first sight this might be thought to be an example of incomplete dominance or codominance between alleles at a single locus. However, when walnut combed birds are crossed together and sufficient progeny are classified, the phenotypes fall into the typical 9:3:3:1 phenotypic ratio of a dihybrid cross. Table 6 shows a Punnett square giving the possible phenotypes of the progeny of crosses amongst walnut combed birds, *Pp Rr* × *Pp Rr*.

Table 6 *Outcome of crosses amongst walnut combed birds*

Gametes from female 'P' locus	'R' locus	Gametes from male			
		P		p	'P' locus
		R	r	R	r	'R' locus
P	R	Walnut	Walnut	Walnut	Walnut
	r	Walnut	Pea	Walnut	Pea
p	R	Walnut	Walnut	Rose	Rose
	r	Walnut	Pea	Rose	Single

3.4.1 Use the data in Table 6 to describe what must appear in the genotype for the phenotype to be
(a) walnut,   (b) pea,   (c) rose,   (d) single.

3.4.2 If the comb shape character were controlled by only one gene locus and walnut is the phenotype of the heterozygote, what would be the result of crossing walnut combed birds? (Remember pea × rose gives walnut.)

Comb shape in poultry is under the control of two gene loci. Like other dihybrid crosses already described, there are four different classes of F_2 progeny and they fall into the phenotypic ratio $9:3:3:1$. Frequently, interaction between genes at different loci causes a modification of this ratio. There are several loci affecting the coat colour of mice. At one locus, known as 'C', there exist the dominant allele for full colour *C* and the recessive allele *c* which, when homozygous, gives rise to the albino (white) phenotype. If the mouse has genotype *CC* or *Cc* then the fur is coloured but what colour it is depends on what alleles are present at locus 'A'. The dominant allele *A* gives agouti colouring. Homozygous recessive *aa* mice lack the yellow band in each hair and are therefore black. If a mouse is homozygous *cc* it will be albino, regardless of whether it is *AA*, *Aa* or *aa* at the 'A' locus. Pigment has to be present before alleles at locus 'A' can affect its distribution. If *Aa Cc* (agouti) mice are crossed amongst themselves, the phenotypes of the offspring will be expected in the ratio **9 agouti : 3 black : 4 albino**.

3.4.3 Construct a Punnett square to show the genotypes of the offspring of a cross between two agouti mice with the genotype *Aa Cc*. Shade the boxes in three colours to correspond with phenotypes agouti, black and albino.

Epistasis is the name given to the type of gene interaction where the expression of alleles at one gene locus is affected by alleles present at another gene locus. In the narrow sense, epistasis means that the presence of certain alleles at one locus prevents the expression of alleles at another. In the mouse *cc* is epistatic to the 'A' locus so mice with the genotype *cc* are always albino. In the broader sense, epistasis refers to any kind of interaction between genes at different loci which affects the way that the genes are expressed in the phenotype. In reality, any aspect of the phenotype is the result of the combined action of many genes. The 'A' locus in the mouse acts in concert with genes at other loci to produce the agouti phenotype, but how many other genes are involved is unknown. Genetic analysis relies on variation; gene loci can only be identified when two or more alleles exist which have recognizably different effects on the phenotype.

Another example of epistasis is in the control of flower colour in the sweet pea. Two varieties of sweet pea have white flowers but they are not genetically the same. Both have, of course, the same gene loci, among them 'C' and 'R' which affect flower colour. One white flowered variety has the genotype *CC rr* and the other is *cc RR*. The development of flower pigment involves a chain of reactions, each step being catalysed by an enzyme. If *C* and *R* each code for a necessary enzyme but *c* and *r* do not, then a plant which is homozygous recessive at either locus will have a break in the chain of reactions leading to flower colour. Thus *cc* is epistatic to the 'R' locus and *rr* is epistatic to the 'C' locus. A plant with the genotype *cc RR* can produce one enzyme and *CC rr* can produce the other. When they are crossed, the progeny (*Cc Rr*) can produce both enzymes and so have coloured flowers. Genes *C* and *R* are said to be **complementary** since both must be present if the flowers are coloured. Together they complete the necessary biochemical pathway. Where epistasis is of the kind just described, the $9:3:3:1$ F_2 phenotypic ratio is modified to **9:7**.

3.4.4 Construct a Punnett square to show the genotypes of the progeny of crosses amongst sweet peas with the genotype *Cc Rr*. Shade the boxes in two colours to correspond with the phenotypes coloured and white.

3.5 *Characters controlled by more than two gene loci*

In this chapter we have seen how a single character like comb shape, fur colour or flower colour can be controlled by two gene loci. Characters which are under the control of one or two loci usually show distinct, qualitatively different traits such as white or coloured, wrinkled or smooth. Indeed, it is often because of the distinct categories of variation that genetic analysis has been carried out. Where a character has a small number of easily distinguished traits, it is said to show **discontinuous variation**.

Much of the variation of interest to plant and animal breeders is not of this kind. The milk yield of cows, for instance, varies between different breeds and between cows of the same breed. Characters like milk yield, egg production in chickens and grain yield in cereals can be measured in some way and are therefore called **quantitative characters**. When variation in a quantitative character is plotted as a frequency distribution (Figure 3) we find that each individual falls somewhere on a continuum which ranges from the lowest to the highest measurement. This kind of variation is described as **continuous**. There are many quantitative human characters such as height, blood pressure and skin colour, all of which show continuous variation.

Figure 3 *Continuous variation in seed weight*

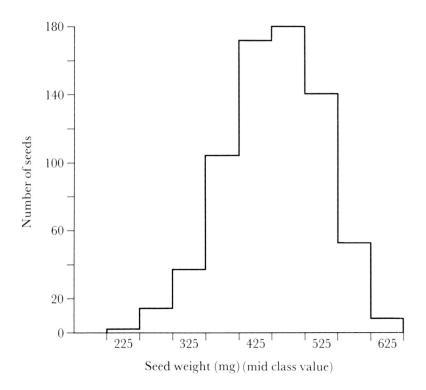

The words discontinuous and continuous are used to describe phenotypic not genotypic variation. Continuous variation can be shown to be related to genetic differences between organisms but the individual genes make a small contribution to the phenotype so that it is difficult to recognize Mendelian ratios. Continuous characters are controlled by many genes, each with a small effect, and for this reason are said to show **polygenic inheritance**. There are methods of analysing polygenic inheritance but they are outside the scope of the present volume.

The number of gene loci controlling a character does not have to be very large before the phenotypic variation can be described as continuous. This is especially true where there is incomplete dominance at each locus. We will consider a hypothetical example. Let us assume that ear length in wheat is controlled by three gene loci, 'A', 'B' and 'C'. There are two alleles at each locus, a and a^1, b and b^1 and c and c^1. Each '1' allele adds 1 cm to the length of the ear and the shortest ears, with genotype *aa bb cc*, are 5 cm. Table 7 shows the genotypes and phenotypes of parental short eared and long eared plants. The F_1 hybrids are heterozygous at all three loci and are intermediate in ear length. Eight kinds of gametes can be produced by the F_1 plants and the Punnett square shows the number of '1' alleles in the genotypes of the F_2 plants.

Table 7 *The results of crossing long eared and short eared wheat (hypothetical example)*

				Parental genotype		*aa bb cc*		$a^1a^1 b^1b^1 c^1c^1$	

Parental genotype   *aa bb cc* $a^1a^1 b^1b^1 c^1c^1$

Phenotype   5 cm   11 cm

F_1 generation genotype $aa^1 bb^1 cc^1$

Phenotype   8 cm

F_2 generation   Gametes from male

		abc	a^1bc	ab^1c	abc^1	a^1b^1c	a^1bc^1	ab^1c^1	$a^1b^1c^1$
	abc	0	1	1	1	2	2	2	3
	a^1bc	1	2	2	2	3	3	3	4
	ab^1c	1	2	2	2	3	3	3	4
Gametes from female	abc^1	1	2	2	2	3	3	3	4
	a^1b^1c	2	3	3	3	4	4	4	5
	a^1bc^1	2	3	3	3	4	4	4	5
	ab^1c^1	2	3	3	3	4	4	4	5
	$a^1b^1c^1$	3	4	4	4	5	5	5	6

3.5.1 Plot a frequency polygon, histogram or bar graph with ear length on the x-axis and number of individuals on the y-axis to show the distribution of ear length in centimetres in the F_2 generation.

This approximately continuous variation which you have plotted has been obtained when only three loci are involved and where each locus has only a small effect on the phenotype. The number of loci and the relative contribution of each locus varies for different characters but in general, continuous characters are controlled by many loci, each with a small effect on the phenotype.

Continuous characters tend to be more susceptible to environmental influences. The milk yield of a cow, for instance, will depend not only on its genotype but also on the quality and amount of food it gets. Of course, environmental influences can also affect discontinuous characters, but not usually enough to blur the distinction between the traits.

3.6 *Summary*

Mendel's experiments with peas demonstrated that the segregation and subsequent inheritance of one pair of alleles is independent of the segregation and inheritance of another pair. This is known as the Law of Independent Assortment and is true when the gene loci involved are on separate pairs of homologous chromosomes.

When two loci control variation in two different characters, a phenotypic ratio of $9:3:3:1$ is obtained in an F_2 generation but this ratio may be modified when both loci control the same character. Such modification occurs when alleles at one locus prevent the expression of alleles at the other. Interaction between alleles at different gene loci is called epistasis and is to be distinguished from dominance and recessivity, interactions between alleles at the same locus.

Characters which show discontinuous variation lend themselves to straightforward genetic analysis and many are found to be under the control of one or two gene loci. Some phenotypic variation ranges from one extreme to another and individuals cannot be easily classified into distinct groups. This kind of variation is generally under the control of many gene loci, each one with a small effect on the phenotype. Such inheritance is described as polygenic and the individual alleles segregate and recombine in just the same way as those with a major phenotypic effect.

Ratios characteristic of dihybrid crosses are

$9:3:3:1$ phenotypic ratio from *Aa Bb* × *Aa Bb*. The ratio is 9 both dominant traits:3 one dominant, one recessive:3 the other dominant, the other recessive:1 both recessive.

$1:1:1:1$ phenotypic ratio from *Aa Bb* × *aa bb* (a backcross or testcross). The ratio is 1 both dominant traits:1 one dominant, one recessive:1 the other dominant, the other recessive:1 both recessive.

$1:1:1:1$ genotypic ratio, again from the cross *Aa Bb* × *aa bb*. The ratio is 1 *Aa Bb*:1 *Aa bb*:1 *aa Bb*:1 *aa bb*.

$9:3:4$ phenotypic ratio from *Aa Bb* × *Aa Bb* where both loci affect the same character and *bb* is epistatic to the 'A' locus. The $\frac{4}{16}$ of the progeny with *bb* all have the same phenotype.

$9:7$ phenotypic ratio from *Aa Bb* × *Aa Bb* where both loci affect the same character. *bb* is epistatic to the 'A' locus and *aa* is epistatic to the 'B' locus. $\frac{9}{16}$ of the progeny have at least one dominant allele at both gene loci and $\frac{7}{16}$ are homozygous recessive at one or both loci.

Key words

	Section		Section
continuous variation	3.5	epistasis	3.4
complementary genes	3.4	Law of Independent	
dihybrid cross	3.1	Assortment	3.1
discontinuous variation	3.5	polygenic inheritance	3.5
double homozygous		quantitative character	3.5
recessive	3.2		

Answers

3.1.1 (a) $\frac{3}{4}$; (b) $\frac{3}{4}$; (c) $\frac{3}{4} \times \frac{3}{4} = \frac{9}{16}$; (d) $\frac{9}{16}$; (e) $\frac{9}{16} \times 556 = 313$ (to nearest whole number); (f) the actual number is 315 which is very close to 313.

3.1.2 (a) 104; (b) 104; (c) 35 (Answers given to nearest whole number.)

3.1.3 (a) Smooth and yellow   *SS YY; SS Yy; Ss YY; Ss Yy*
Smooth and green   *SS yy; Ss yy*
Wrinkled and yellow   *ss YY; ss Yy*
Wrinkled and green   *ss yy.*
(b) 9 smooth, yellow : 3 smooth, green : 3 wrinkled, yellow : 1 wrinkled, green.

3.1.4 (a) $\frac{1}{4}$; (b) $\frac{1}{2}$; (c) $\frac{1}{4} \times \frac{1}{2} = \frac{1}{8}$; (d) $\frac{2}{16} = \frac{1}{8}$ are *SS Yy*.

3.2.1 (a) $\frac{1}{2}$ *Aa Bb* and $\frac{1}{2}$ *Aa bb*; (b) $\frac{1}{2}$ *Tt zz* and $\frac{1}{2}$ *tt zz*;
(c) $\frac{1}{4}$ *Gg Hh*, $\frac{1}{4}$ *Gg hh*, $\frac{1}{4}$ *gg Hh*, $\frac{1}{4}$ *gg hh*.

3.4.1 (a) *R* and *P*; (b) *P* and *rr*; (c) *R* and *pp*; (d) *pp rr*.

3.4.2 1 pea : 2 walnut : 1 rose.

3.4.3 Agouti   *AA CC; AA Cc; Aa CC; Aa Cc*
Black   *aa CC; aa Cc*
Albino   *AA cc; Aa cc; aa cc*

3.4.4 Coloured   *CC RR; CC Rr; Cc RR; Cc Rr*
White   *cc RR; cc Rr; CC rr; Cc rr; cc rr*

PROBLEMS

26 (a) The cross *AA BB* × *aa bb* gives progeny with the genotype *Aa Bb*. What other cross will give all progeny with this same genotype?
(b) The cross *Aa Bb* × *aa bb* will give an expected ratio of 1 *Aa Bb* : 1 *aa Bb* : 1 *Aa bb* : 1 *aa bb* in the progeny. What other cross will give the same genotypic ratio?

(c) Using gene loci 'A' and 'B' state the genotypes which must be crossed in order to obtain a phenotypic ratio of $9:3:3:1$ in the progeny.

27 Grey seed coat (testa) colour in peas is dominant to white and tall stem is dominant to short.
   (a) If pure breeding tall plants which bear white seeds (genotype $TT\,gg$) are crossed with pure breeding short plants which bear grey seeds ($tt\,GG$), what will be the phenotype of the F_1?
   (b) If the F_1 plants are selfed, what will be the expected phenotypes in the F_2 generation and in what ratios are they likely to occur?

28 Tomato plants heterozygous for the recessive traits 'potato leaf' (c) and hairless (h) are selfed and the seeds are collected. Use the probability method to calculate the proportions of the progeny with
   (a) the genotype $Cc\,Hh$;   (b) the phenotype normal leaf, hairless.

29 The following cross was made between two tomato plants (see previous question for symbols)
$$Cc\,hh \times Cc\,Hh$$
Using the probability method, calculate the expected proportion of the progeny with
   (a) the genotype $CC\,hh$;   (b) the phenotype potato leaf, hairless.

30 Crosses between White Leghorn fowl with single combs and white feathers and Indian Game fowl with pea combs and dark feathers produced white, pea combed F_1 progeny. When the F_1 birds were crossed amongst themselves the F_2 progeny appeared in the ratio
   9 white, pea : 3 white, single : 3 dark, pea : 1 dark, single
One white, single combed cock from the F_2 generation is then crossed to several single combed, dark feathered hens. What is the probability that the cock would have only white offspring?

31 In budgerigars, one gene locus controls the general colouring of the feathers with green being dominant to blue. A second gene locus controls the intensity of the colouring. The intensity in the heterozygote is intermediate between that of the homozygotes. The names of the six possible phenotypes are given in the table.

	Intensity		
General colour	Pale	Mid	Dark
Green	Light green	Dark green	Olive
Blue	Sky blue	Cobalt	Mauve

In the following crosses, suggest genotypes for the parents and the expected proportions of the phenotypes of their offspring.
   (a) Homozygous light green × cobalt;

(b) heterozygous olive × heterozygous olive;

(c) heterozygous dark green × cobalt.

32 In the Andalusian fowl, the allele for black feathers is incompletely dominant to that for white feathers and the phenotype of the heterozygote is described as blue. The texture of the feathers is controlled by a second gene locus, silky feathers being recessive to normal. Crosses were made amongst blue birds heterozygous at the *silky* locus. What offspring phenotypic ratios would be expected?

33 In the tomato, yellow flower is dominant to white and tall is dominant to dwarf. A certain plant was allowed to self fertilize and produced offspring in the ratio

9 yellow, tall : 3 yellow, dwarf : 3 white, tall : 1 white, dwarf

The yellow, dwarf and white, tall plants were discarded. All of the tall, yellow flowered plants were pollinated using pollen from dwarf, white flowered plants. What proportion of the tall, yellow flowered plants would yield the following progeny?

(a) All yellow, tall;   (b) $\frac{1}{2}$ yellow, tall and $\frac{1}{2}$ yellow, dwarf;

(c) $\frac{1}{4}$ yellow, tall, $\frac{1}{4}$ yellow, dwarf, $\frac{1}{4}$ white, tall and $\frac{1}{4}$ white, dwarf;

(d) $\frac{1}{2}$ yellow, tall and $\frac{1}{2}$ white, tall.

34 From a certain cross between pea plants differing in two seed characters, Mendel found the following results:

55 smooth, yellow

51 smooth, green

49 wrinkled, yellow

52 wrinkled, green

Yellow is dominant to green and smooth is dominant to wrinkled. What were the genotypes of the parents of this generation? List all possible answers and define gene symbols.

35 There is an inherited disease in humans called phenylketonuria which is caused by a recessive mutant allele. Two parents are heterozygous for this condition. One parent has blood group O and the other has blood group AB. What is the probability that their child will have blood group A and phenylketonuria?

36 The eyes of wild type *Drosophila* contain both a red and a brown pigment and they appear dark red. Flies with the genotype *st/st* have scarlet eyes (bright red) because they fail to make the brown pigment. Flies with the genotype *bw/bw* have brown eyes because they fail to make the red pigment. Eyes with no pigment at all are white. In the following crosses, give the phenotypes of the parents and the expected proportions of the phenotypes of their offspring.

(a) *bw/bw st/st* × *Bw/bw St/st*;   (b) *Bw/bw St/st* × *Bw/bw St/st*;

(c) *Bw/bw st/st* × *bw/bw St/St*.

37 There is a mutant form of *Drosophila* known as 'gouty legs' which has short, thick legs. The allele controlling the trait (*gy*) is recessive to wild type. The following cross was made:

wild type eye colour, gouty legs × wild type eye colour, wild type legs

The progeny obtained were:

27 wild type eye colour, wild type legs

18 wild type eye colour, gouty legs

5 scarlet eye colour, wild type legs

10 scarlet eye colour, gouty legs

What were the most likely genotypes of the parents?

38 The Irish setter is normally red although black animals are known. Several gene loci affect coat colour, including 'A' and 'E'. The dominant allele *A* is epistatic to the 'E' locus such that the presence of allele *A* always gives rise to a red coat. The homozygous recessive condition at the 'E' locus also produces a red coat. Other genotypes give black. Two double heterozygous animals are crossed. What is the probability that they will produce a black pup?

39 Some plants of the white clover *Trifolium repens* produce hydrogen cyanide (HCN) when damaged and are said to be cyanogenic. Acyanogenic plants do not produce HCN. Cyanogenesis depends on the presence in the leaves of certain glucosides which can be broken down to release HCN. The presence of these glucosides is controlled by the dominant allele *Ac*. The genotype of the acyanogenic plants is *ac/ac*. Cyanogenesis also depends on the presence of an enzyme, linamarase, which breaks down the glucosides. The presence of linamarase is controlled by the dominant allele *Li*. Plants with the genotype *li/li* produce no linamarase. In an experiment, 1600 plants were collected, being the progeny of crosses amongst *Ac/ac Li/li* plants.

(a) How many plants would be expected to be cyanogenic and how many acyanogenic?

(b) Leaves from the acyanogenic plants were individually crushed, and purified glucosides were added. How many of these plants would now produce HCN?

(c) Leaves from the acyanogenic plants were again individually crushed and the purified enzyme linamarase was added. How many of these plants would now produce HCN?

(d) How many plants would be expected to remain acyanogenic after either treatment?

40 In the dachshund there are two gene loci 'W' and 'K' which affect hair type. The presence of *W* results in wire hair. The phenotypes were recorded of a large number of offspring of crosses between wire haired animals with the genotype *Ww Kk* and the ratio was found to be

12 wire haired : 3 short haired : 1 long haired

When crossed amongst themselves, long haired animals have only long haired puppies.

(a) What genotype(s) give(s)   (i) long hair,   (ii) short hair?

(b) Frank Furter, a wire haired dog, was crossed to several long haired bitches and the phenotypes of the puppies were in the approximate ratio

1 long haired : 2 wire haired : 1 short haired

What was Frank's genotype?

4 Sex determination and sex linkage

4.1 Sex determination

Most animals and some plants are either males or females and the sex is normally genetically determined. (The sex of some reptiles is influenced by the temperature at which the eggs develop.) Mosquitoes exhibit the simplest genetic sex determining mechanism, a single locus with two alleles. Males are heterozygous and females are homozygous recessive. Because matings are always between these two genotypes, the ratio of males to females is $1:1$. This ratio is achieved in other animals by the segregation of a pair of chromosomes, the **sex chromosomes**. The two sexes carry different chromosome complements or **karyotypes**. The chromosomes which are not involved with sex determination are called **autosomes**, of which males and females have the same kind and number (except *Hymenoptera*, see below).

A chromosome associated with sex was first discovered in the male of a species of bug. At first it was not certain whether it was a chromosome and, unlike all the other chromosomes, it was found in only half of the males' sperm. It was an 'unknown quantity' and for this reason was called 'X'. A few years later, in a species of beetle, another chromosome was discovered which paired with the X, so this one was called 'Y'.

In humans and *Drosophila*, females possess two X-chromosomes and males possess an X and a Y. The karyotype of a female is therefore two sets of autosomes plus XX and the karyotype of a male is two sets of autosomes plus XY (see Figure 1). In a female the two X-chromosomes are homologous, but in most mammals the Y-chromosome is much smaller. However, in *Drosophila*, the Y is longer than the X and is hook shaped. The X- and Y-chromosomes pair at meiosis because they have a homologous pairing segment. The non-pairing region is called the **differential segment**. There are genes in this differential segment of the X-chromosome which are not present on the Y. In fact the Y-chromosome in most species has very few known genes although it is not without function.

The sex chromosomes pair during meiosis prophase I and then segregate at anaphase I. This means that, in males, one product of the first meiotic division (a secondary spermatocyte) receives an X and the other receives a Y. The second meiotic division separates the chromatids so two spermatids get an X and two get a Y. Thus 50% of the sperm carry

Figure 1 *Normal human chromosome complements*

(a) Male

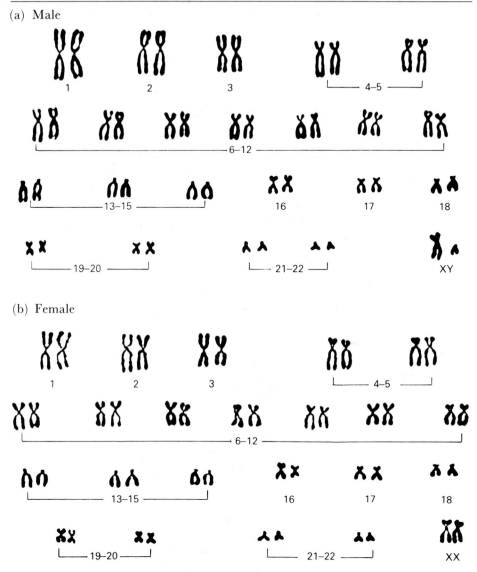

(b) Female

Both sexes have two copies of each of the autosomes (numbers 1–22) and a pair of sex chromosomes. These pictures are called karyograms and are prepared from photographs of human white blood cells undergoing mitosis. A photograph is selected where all the chromosomes are visible and not overlapping. (See the example in chapter 5, figure 8.) The chromosomes are cut out, matched and stuck down in pairs in order of size. Note: although the shapes of the sex chromosomes resemble the letters X and Y, that is not the reason they were so named.

an X and 50% carry a Y. Female gametes all carry one X-chromosome. (See Figure 2.) On fertilization, the ovum has an equal chance of fusing with an X-bearing or a Y-bearing sperm. The karyotype of the zygote is

Figure 2 *Segregation of sex chromosomes in human gametogenesis*

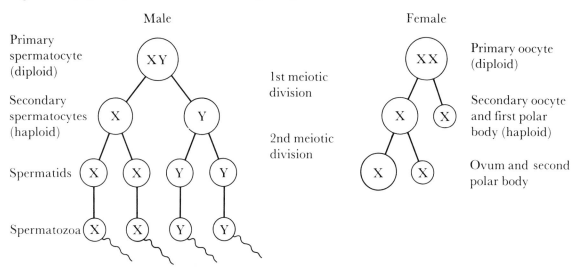

therefore autosomes plus either XX (female) or XY (male), the two types occurring in equal numbers.

For the first seven weeks of development, the human embryo displays no external indication of its sex. The gonads at this stage are capable of developing into either ovaries or testes. Their hormonal environment determines their fate. The Y-chromosome acts as a switch; its presence in the body cells causes the gonads to develop into testes, while in its absence, the gonads develop into ovaries. Presumably the Y-chromosome gives rise to a higher level of male hormones and it is this which brings about testicular development. An interesting condition exists where a person is genetically XY but phenotypically female because the gonads have failed to respond to the presence of male hormones during development. The condition is called testicular feminization and it is due to a mutant allele of a gene which normally codes for an enzyme concerned with the metabolism of testosterone in the cells.

The switch mechanism of the Y-chromosome is demonstrated by the phenotypes associated with certain abnormal human karyotypes. Occasionally, the sex chromosomes do not segregate as they should and the products of meiosis receive both or neither. Abnormal sperm can contain both an X- and a Y-chromosome and abnormal ova can contain two X-chromosomes. Sometimes a gamete contains no sex chromosome at all. If a normal ovum is fertilized by an XY sperm the zygote will be XXY. If two gametes fuse, one of which has no sex chromosome, the zygote will have either one X or one Y. In such cells, the absence of a sex chromosome is designated by a 0 (zero). Y0 zygotes die very early in development but some X0 zygotes survive. About 5% of human X0 foetuses conceived survive to birth and beyond. There is no appreciable increase in prenatal mortality associated with the XXY karyotype.

Like males, X0 individuals have only one X-chromosome but their phenotype is female while XXY individuals are males even though they have two X-chromosomes. Both abnormal karyotypes lead to sterility and each is associated with a syndrome of other characteristic features. Normal males are males therefore because they have a Y-chromosome, not because they have only one X. These observations support the idea that the presence of a Y-chromosome switches development into the male pathway. In the absence of a Y, development proceeds along the female pathway – at least in humans.

In some insects such as grasshoppers, there is no Y-chromosome at all. X0 individuals are normal, fertile males, and the normal female is XX. As well as sex chromosomes, both males and females have two sets of autosomes, as in other species. In *Hymenoptera* (ants, bees and wasps), no sex chromosomes have been identified and sex determination is unusual. A fertile female or 'queen' is able to lay either fertilized, diploid eggs or unfertilized, haploid eggs. The diploid ones develop into females and the haploid ones into males so male *Hymenoptera* have a mother but no father. They are one of the rare examples of haploid animals.

In all the species so far described (except *Hymenoptera*), all the female's gametes carry the same kind of sex chromosome and so females are called the **homogametic sex**. Males produce two different types of gametes and are therefore known as the **heterogametic sex**. In birds, butterflies and moths however, it is the female which is the heterogametic sex (XY) and the homogametic sex is the male (XX).

The sex chromosome complement of an individual determines what sex it will be but it must be realized that the sex chromosomes do not carry all the genes responsible for sexual characteristics. Although there is some evidence that the human X-chromosome carries genes for female fertility and the *Drosophila* Y-chromosome carries genes for male fertility there is no evidence that genes controlling the structure of the genitalia, for instance, are on the sex chromosomes. Both sexes possess genes for features characteristic of the opposite sex. In mammals, whether or not those genes are expressed depends on the level of male hormones present and this in turn depends on the presence or absence of the Y-chromosome. This is illustrated by the inheritance of baldness in humans. The pattern of inheritance is consistent with control by a single locus with two alleles B and B'. BB homozygotes in both sexes do not become bald. $B'B'$ homozygotes become bald, whatever the sex. $B'B$ males become bald but $B'B$ females do not. Hair growth is under the influence of sex hormones and where there is a high level of male sex hormones, heterozygotes lose their head hair although facial hair continues to grow. A woman with a tumour of the adrenal cortex also produces high levels of male hormones so becomes bald if she is a heterozygote and will also develop a beard. Although she is a woman her male hormone level allows the expression of genes normally expressed only in males.

4.2   *Sex linkage in* **Drosophila** *and humans*

In the examples of monohybrid and dihybrid crosses given in previous chapters, the same outcome was expected from both reciprocal crosses. This is not always the case, however. In *Drosophila*, the allele for white eyes, w, is recessive to the wild type allele W, which gives red eyes. The results of two reciprocal crosses are given in Table 1.

Table 1   *The outcome of two reciprocal* Drosophila *crosses*

(a)   Parents: Homozygous red eyed female × white eyed male
       Progeny: Red eyed males and females

(b)   Parents: White eyed female × red eyed male
       Progeny: Red eyed females and white eyed males

The explanation for such observations is that the *white* locus is on the differential segment of the X-chromosome. Males have only one X-chromosome so any recessive allele on it in this region will be expressed. Males can be neither homozygous nor heterozygous for genes on the X; they are said to be **hemizygous**. Males receive their X-chromosome from their mother. In part (b) of Table 1 the F_1 males have received the w allele from their mother and are therefore white eyed. Their sisters receive w from their mother and W on the X-chromosome from their father. They are heterozygous and therefore red eyed. A trait which can be shown by both sexes but whose inheritance is linked with the inheritance of sex is said to be **sex linked**. The traits which show this kind of inheritance are almost always controlled by a gene on the X-chromosome. Such a gene is sex linked. There are very few examples of sex linked genes which are on the Y-chromosome but, to distinguish the two, we can use the terms **X-linked** and **Y-linked**. However, in the absence of any other information, sex linked means X-linked. Sex linked inheritance of eye colour in *Drosophila* is illustrated in Figure 3.

In problems involving sex linkage, an individual's sex chromosomes are indicated as well as its genotype. This notation is used in Table 2 which shows the same crosses as Table 1 and a further generation. It is apparent from the F_2 generation in Table 2 that the offspring phenotypic ratios differ according to whether a heterozygous female is crossed with a red eyed male or with a white eyed male. In Table 2, the ratio in the F_2 generation of cross (b) would also be expected even if *white* were not sex linked (i.e. $Ww \times ww$ would give a ratio of 1 red eyed : 1 white eyed with equal numbers of males and females in both phenotypic classes). However, when $X^W X^w$ and $X^W Y$ are crossed, all the females and half the males are red eyed and the other half of the males are white eyed. The phenotypic ratio is different in males and females.

Figure 3 *Sex linked inheritance of red and white eyes in* Drosophila

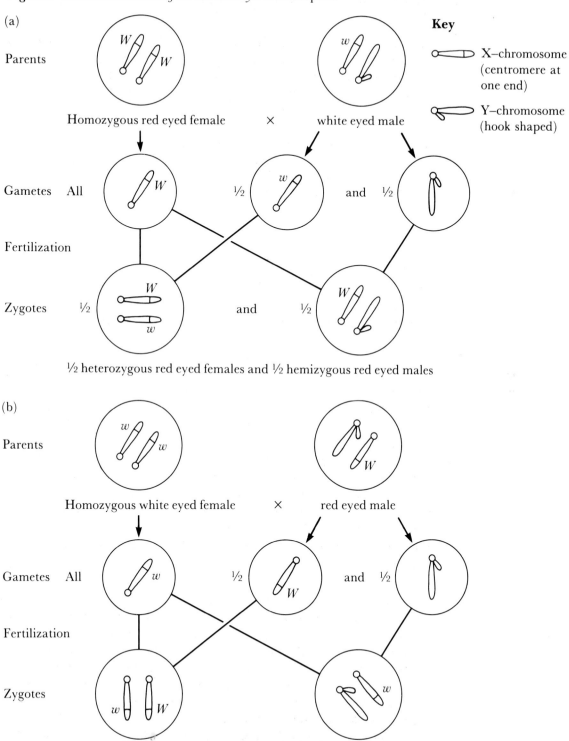

(a)

Parents

Homozygous red eyed female × white eyed male

Key

X–chromosome (centromere at one end)

Y–chromosome (hook shaped)

Gametes All ½ and ½

Fertilization

Zygotes ½ and ½

½ heterozygous red eyed females and ½ hemizygous red eyed males

(b)

Parents

Homozygous white eyed female × red eyed male

Gametes All ½ and ½

Fertilization

Zygotes

½ heterozygous red eyed females and ½ hemizygous white eyed males

Table 2 *Two reciprocal* Drosophila *crosses showing genotypes*

(a)	$X^W X^W$	×	$X^w Y$		(b)	$X^w X^w$	×	$X^W Y$
	Red eyed female		white eyed male			White eyed female		red eyed male

		Gametes from male				Gametes from male
		$\frac{1}{2} X^w$	$\frac{1}{2} Y$			$\frac{1}{2} X^W$	$\frac{1}{2} Y$
Gametes from female	All X^W	$\frac{1}{2} X^W X^w$	$\frac{1}{2} X^W Y$	Gametes from female	All X^w	$\frac{1}{2} X^w X^W$	$\frac{1}{2} X^w Y$
		Red F_1 females	Red F_1 males			Red F_1 females	White F_1 males

		Gametes from F_1 male				Gametes from F_1 male
		$\frac{1}{2} X^W$	$\frac{1}{2} Y$			$\frac{1}{2} X^w$	$\frac{1}{2} Y$
Gametes from F_1 female	$\frac{1}{2} X^W$ $\frac{1}{2} X^w$	$\frac{1}{4} X^W X^W$ $\frac{1}{4} X^w X^W$	$\frac{1}{4} X^W Y$ $\frac{1}{4} X^w Y$	Gametes from F_1 female	$\frac{1}{2} X^W$ $\frac{1}{2} X^w$	$\frac{1}{4} X^W X^w$ $\frac{1}{4} X^w X^w$	$\frac{1}{4} X^W Y$ $\frac{1}{4} X^w Y$

F_2 phenotypes:

$\frac{1}{2}$ red eyed females ($X^W X^w$ and $X^W X^W$) $\frac{1}{4}$ red eyed females ($X^W X^w$)
$\frac{1}{4}$ red eyed males ($X^W Y$) $\frac{1}{4}$ white eyed females ($X^w X^w$)
$\frac{1}{4}$ white eyed males ($X^w Y$) $\frac{1}{4}$ red eyed males ($X^W Y$)
  $\frac{1}{4}$ white eyed males ($X^w Y$)

Notice the way that the sex chromosomes and therefore the sex linked genes are passed from parents to offspring. Boys always inherit their Y-chromosome from their father. If a particular trait is always passed from father to son and is never shown by females it is probable that the gene involved is on the Y-chromosome (assuming the trait is controlled by a single gene). The only reasonably well-documented case of Y-linkage in humans is hairy ears, where long hairs grow on the upper part of the pinna. Males always inherit their X-chromosome from their mother and pass it on to their daughters. This sometimes leads to what may be called 'criss-cross' inheritance of a sex linked trait. This type of inheritance is illustrated in Figure 4. 'Criss-cross' inheritance of sex linked genes does not always occur because females can pass the gene to their daughters as well as to their sons.

Sex linkage is the reason that several abnormal conditions in humans are more frequently observed in males than in females. If a female carries a recessive, sex linked mutant allele, she is likely to have a normal allele on her other sex chromosome and she will be unaffected. Any male carrying such a mutant allele has no second X-chromosome and will therefore show the mutant phenotype. Recessive sex linked traits include red–green colour-blindness affecting about 8% of males but only 0·7% of

Figure 4 *'Criss-cross' inheritance of a sex linked trait*

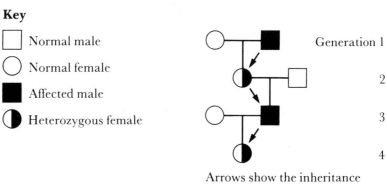

Key

☐ Normal male

◯ Normal female

■ Affected male

◖ Heterozygous female

Generation 1

2

3

4

Arrows show the inheritance
of the X–chromosome

females, haemophilia affecting one in 10 000 males but almost unknown in females, and forms of diabetes insipidus and muscular dystrophy. The fact that these mutant alleles are X-linked means that the X-chromosome carries genes which are necessary for normal colour vision, blood clotting, antidiuretic hormone production and muscle development, all of which are functions of both sexes. This illustrates the important fact that sex linked genes do not necessarily affect sexual characters. The genes controlling these are mainly on the autosomes.

4.2.1   A female *Drosophila*, heterozygous for the recessive allele for yellow body colour, is mated to a wild type (grey bodied) male who does not carry the *yellow* allele. Use the Punnett square method to show the genotypes and phenotypes of their progeny
(a) if *yellow* is not sex linked, and (b) if *yellow* is sex linked.
(Hint: use letters other than *Y* and *y* to represent alleles at the *yellow* locus to avoid confusion with the Y-chromosome.)

4.2.2   In *Drosophila*, *yellow* is sex linked. What would be the phenotypes and genotypes of the parents in a cross which gave all yellow males and all wild type females in the progeny?

4.3   *Inactivation of X-chromosomes*

As far as autosomes are concerned, both members of a pair of homologues make gene products, but the situation is different with the sex chromosomes. In female mammals it is thought that only one X-chromosome is functional in each cell. The other remains highly condensed and inactive. Whether it is the maternal or paternal X which is inactivated is random, so a female is a mosaic of cells, some of which have only an active paternal X-chromosome and others which have only an active maternal X-chromosome. The inactivation occurs early in development so the mosaic is a coarse one, i.e. patches of the body have the same active X-chromosome. This leads to an interesting phenomenon in domestic cats where coat colour is affected by an X-linked gene. $X^G X^G$ and $X^G Y$ are ginger females and males respectively, $X^g X^g$ and $X^g Y$ are tabby, black or another colour, whichever is determined by genes on the autosomes. We will use black in our example. The third possible female genotype is $X^G X^g$. In patches of her body, X^G will be active and the fur will be ginger while in other patches the X^g chromosome will be the active one, making the fur black. This patchy colouring is called tortoiseshell and occurs only in females. Male tortoiseshell cats are very rare and are always sterile because they have the karyotype XXY.

An inactivated X-chromosome readily takes up aceto-orcein stain and can easily be seen in the nucleus of cells from the cheek lining as a small dark area. It is called a **Barr body** after its discoverer and occurs only in nuclei containing more than one X-chromosome. A straightforward means of discovering the sex of an unborn child is to examine some foetal cells taken from the amniotic fluid surrounding it. The number of Barr bodies visible in a cell is one fewer than the number of X chromosomes.

4.3.1 A single Barr body was visible in the cells of an unborn child.
(a) What sex would you expect this child to be?
(b) The child was in fact male. Show his sex chromosome constitution.

4.3.2 A Barr body is usually visible in about 30% of cells taken from the cheek lining of a female. A girl could find no Barr body in any of her cells. What may be her sex chromosome constitution?

4.4 Summary

In many diploid species, both sexes carry two sets of autosomes but differ in their possession of another pair of chromosomes called the sex chromosomes. These determine the individual's sex but they do not necessarily carry genes which control sexual characteristics.

In mammals and *Drosophila*, the female possesses two X-chromosomes in each somatic cell and is called the homogametic sex. The male has both an X- and a Y-chromosome and is called the heterogametic sex because he produces 50% X-bearing and 50% Y-bearing gametes. In birds, butterflies and moths, the female is the heterogametic sex.

Genes located on the sex chromosomes are described as sex linked but in most species the Y-chromosome carries few known genes. The heterogametic sex carries only one X-chromosome and so all of its genes which have no corresponding allele on the Y-chromosome will be expressed in the phenotype. As a consequence, characters controlled by sex linked genes (sex linked characters) may show the following modes of inheritance.

(a) Two reciprocal crosses give different results in the F_1 generation.

(b) The phenotypic ratio differs in the male and female progeny of a cross.

(c) A trait shows 'criss-cross' inheritance.

(d) A trait is more common amongst the heterogametic sex than amongst the homogametic sex.

A cell, whether male or female, has only one functional X-chromosome. If two X-chromosomes are present, as in a female mammal, one remains condensed and inactive. In some cells the active one is the maternal homologue and in others it is the paternal homologue. The inactivated X-chromosome is visible in stained nuclei and is called a Barr body.

Key words

	Section		Section
autosome	4.1	sex chromosomes	4.1
Barr body	4.3	sex linked	4.2
differential segment	4.1	X-chromosome	4.1
hemizygous	4.2	X-linked	4.2
heterogametic sex	4.1	Y-chromosome	4.1
homogametic sex	4.1	Y-linked	4.2
karyotype	4.1		

Answers

4.2.1 (a) If *yellow* is not sex linked, the female parent is *Cc* and the male is *CC*.

		Gametes from female	
		$\frac{1}{2}C$	$\frac{1}{2}c$
Gametes from male	All C	$\frac{1}{2}CC$	$\frac{1}{2}Cc$

So the offspring are all wild type.

(b) If *yellow* is sex linked, the female parent is $X^C X^c$ and the male is $X^C Y$.

		Gametes from female	
		$\frac{1}{2}X^C$	$\frac{1}{2}X^c$
Gametes from male	$\frac{1}{2}X^C$	$\frac{1}{4}X^C X^C$	$\frac{1}{4}X^C X^c$
	$\frac{1}{2}Y$	$\frac{1}{4}X^C Y$	$\frac{1}{4}X^c Y$

All the female progeny are wild type ($X^C X^C$ and $X^C X^c$). Half the males are wild type ($X^C Y$) and half are yellow ($X^c Y$).

4.2.2   For the male progeny to be yellow, they must all inherit X^c from their mother so the female parent must be yellow and have the genotype $X^c X^c$. The female offspring will also receive X^c from their mother. They are wild type so have received X^C from their father who therefore has the genotype $X^C Y$ and is wild type.

4.3.1   (a) Female;   (b) XXY.

4.3.2   X0.

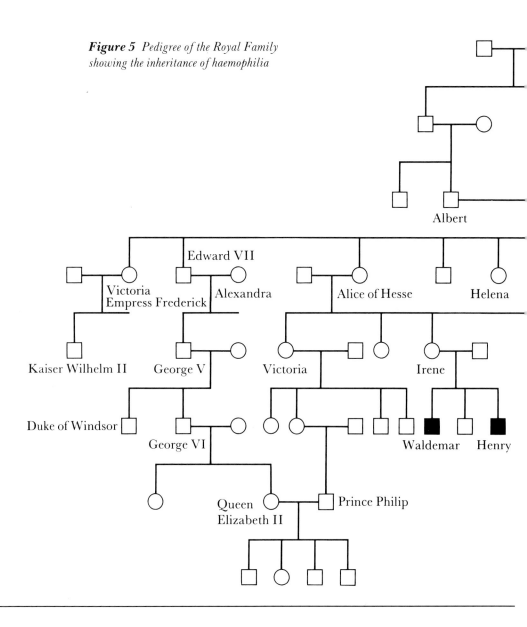

Figure 5 *Pedigree of the Royal Family showing the inheritance of haemophilia*

PROBLEMS

41 The wild type body colour in *Drosophila* is grey and is dominant to yellow. When a yellow female fly was mated to a wild type male, all the F_1 male progeny were yellow and all the F_1 female progeny were wild type. The F_1 progeny were allowed to interbreed. Show the two crosses diagrammatically and state the expected ratio of wild type to yellow in the male and female F_2 progeny.

42 Haemophilia is caused by a recessive sex linked gene. Figure 5 shows the inheritance of the disease in descendants of Queen Victoria. Name the females in this pedigree who are certain to be heterozygous.

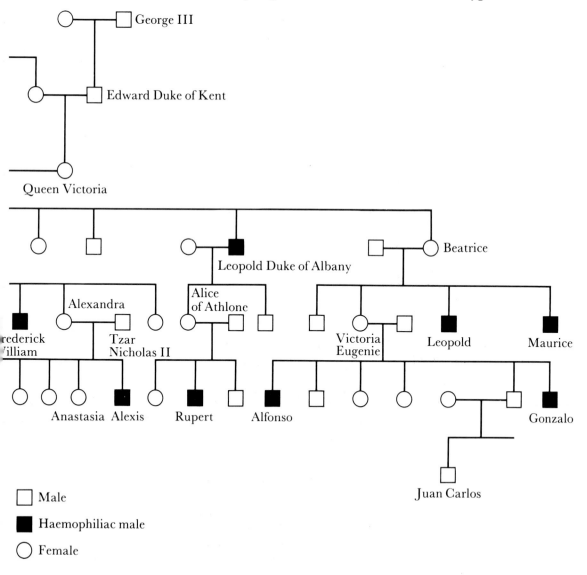

□ Male

■ Haemophiliac male

○ Female

43 The blood of haemophiliacs clots very slowly and they also suffer from bleeding in the joints. Female haemophiliacs are rarely born. What would be the most likely genotypes of the parents of such a female?

44 Red–green colour-blindness is caused by a sex linked gene and is recessive to normal colour vision. A boy has inherited colour-blindness from one of his grandfathers. Is the affected grandparent his mother's or his father's father?

45 A woman's brother died of Duchenne's muscular dystrophy which is caused by a recessive sex linked gene.
  (a) In the absence of any further information, what is the probability that she is heterozygous (i.e. a carrier) for this disease?
  (b) She marries and has a son who also suffers from the disease. What is the probability that a second son will be affected in the same way?

46 The phenotypes and genotypes of certain coat colours in cats is shown in the table below.

	Genotype	
Phenotype	Male	Female
Black	X^gY	X^gX^g
Ginger	X^GY	X^GX^G
Tortoiseshell	—	X^GX^g

A breeder has a number of black, ginger and tortoiseshell cats.
  (a) If she wants all the female kittens to be tortoiseshell, what are the genotypes and phenotypes of the parents she should use? List all possible answers.
  (b) What will be the phenotypes of the male kittens in the crosses you have suggested?
  (c) Suggest a reason to account for the appearance of an infertile black female in the litter of a cross between a ginger tom and a black female.

47 A female *Drosophila* with the mutant phenotype 'notched wings' was mated to a wild type male. Two-thirds of the progeny were female. Half of the females had notched wings and the other half had wild type wings and all the male progeny had wild type wings. When the notched progeny were mated to their wild type brothers, the same results were obtained. Explain.

In your answers to questions 48, 49 and 50 remember that in birds and moths the female is the heterogametic sex.

48 Sexing newly hatched chicks is tedious. In the Plymouth Rock breed of fowl there is a dominant sex linked gene *B* which causes the normally black feathers to have a white bar. Newly hatched chicks which carry the

B allele can be recognized by a white spot on the head. What parent birds should a poultry breeder use in order to be able to quickly distinguish between males and females soon after hatching?

49 The wing markings of budgerigars are normally black. The sex linked gene *cinnamon* causes brown colouration and is recessive to the allele for black. A breeder possesses a number of birds, none of which carries the *cinnamon* allele. He purchases a cinnamon female. Illustrate by means of diagrams the breeding programme he should carry out in order to obtain, in as few generations as possible, birds which have only cinnamon progeny of both sexes. Bear in mind that budgies live for several years and can breed every year.

50 There is a rare black form of the Pale Brindled Beauty moth. All the moths of this type are female and all their female offspring are black while their sons are normal. With the help of diagrams explain these observations.

5 Genes and chromosomes

5.1 Linked genes

The $3:1$ F_2 phenotypic ratio and the $1:1$ backcross ratio in a monohybrid cross are a consequence of both the segregation of alleles at gamete formation and the random fusion of gametes. The dihybrid ratios $9:3:3:1$ and $1:1:1:1$ are a result of the independent segregation of alleles at the two gene loci and the random fusion of gametes. Early experiments soon revealed pairs of characters whose inheritance did not obey the Law of Independent Assortment because the ratios expected of a dihybrid cross were not obtained. In fact no consistent ratios were found. In one experiment Bateson and Punnett crossed a homozygous purple flowered sweet pea having long pollen grains (*FF LL*) with a red flowered plant having round pollen grains (*ff ll*). The F_1 plants were purple flowered and had long pollen (*Ff Ll*). When the F_1 plants were selfed, the expected phenotypic ratio of $9:3:3:1$ was not observed.

Table 1 shows that long pollen grains tend to be inherited with purple flower and round pollen with red flower. The traits which are present together in the parental generation tend to be passed on together to the F_2 generation. The frequency of occurrence of new combinations is not as great as expected on the basis of Mendel's second law. The reason that traits sometimes tend to be inherited together is that the loci of the genes controlling them are on the same chromosome. Such gene loci are said to be **linked**. The loci will always remain on the same chromosome unless a very rare event separates them (e.g. translocation; see section 5.7). Linked genes do not normally become unlinked.

In a diploid organism there are two copies of each chromosome, i.e. the chromosomes are present in homologous pairs. Two loci which are linked on one homologue are therefore also linked on the other, so it is correct to say either that genes which are linked are on the same

Table 1 *The results of Bateson and Punnett's experiment*

Phenotype	Observed	Expected
Purple flower, long pollen	296	240
Purple flower, round pollen	19	80
Red flower, long pollen	27	80
Red flower, round pollen	85	27

chromosome or that genes which are linked are on the same pair of homologous chromosomes.

An individual heterozygous at two gene loci (the double heterozygote) has two different alleles at both loci. If the gene loci are linked, the alleles may be linked in two different ways as shown in Figure 1.

Figure 1 *Linkage of genes 'A' and 'B'*

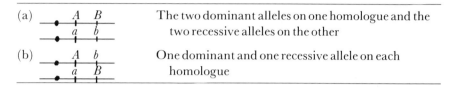

(a)	$\dfrac{A \quad B}{a \quad b}$	The two dominant alleles on one homologue and the two recessive alleles on the other
(b)	$\dfrac{A \quad b}{a \quad B}$	One dominant and one recessive allele on each homologue

The conventional way of representing the genotype of a double heterozygote is *Aa Bb* and this method can also be used when the genes are known to be linked. But if it is desired to indicate that fact, the

Table 2 *Bateson and Punnett's experiment with sweet peas*

Parents' phenotype	Purple flower, long pollen	Red flower, round pollen
Parents' genotype	$\dfrac{F \; L}{F \; L}$	$\dfrac{f \; l}{f \; l}$
Gametes' genotype	$\underline{F \; L}$	$\underline{f \; l}$
F₁ genotype	$\dfrac{F \; L}{f \; l}$	
F₁ phenotype	Purple flower, long pollen	

F₂ genotypes

Gametes from F₁ males

Gametes from F₁ females	$\underline{F\;L}$	$\underline{f\;l}$	$\underline{F\;l}$	$\underline{f\;L}$
$\underline{F\;L}$	$\dfrac{F\;L}{F\;L}$	$\dfrac{f\;l}{F\;L}$	$\dfrac{F\;l}{F\;L}$	$\dfrac{f\;L}{F\;L}$
$\underline{f\;l}$	$\dfrac{F\;L}{f\;l}$	$\dfrac{f\;l}{f\;l}$	$\dfrac{F\;l}{f\;l}$	$\dfrac{f\;L}{f\;l}$
$\underline{F\;l}$	$\dfrac{F\;L}{F\;l}$	$\dfrac{f\;l}{F\;l}$	$\dfrac{F\;l}{F\;l}$	$\dfrac{f\;L}{F\;l}$
$\underline{f\;L}$	$\dfrac{F\;L}{f\;L}$	$\dfrac{f\;l}{f\;L}$	$\dfrac{F\;l}{f\;L}$	$\dfrac{f\;L}{f\;L}$

genotype can be shown as a shorthand version of a chromosome diagram,

i.e. $\dfrac{A\ \ B}{a\ \ b}$ or $\dfrac{A\ \ b}{a\ \ B}$. This notation is used in Table 2 which explains the sweet pea cross.

In Bateson and Punnett's results there was a deficiency of the genotypes shown in the shaded part of the table and an excess of the genotypes shown in the unshaded part. This is because gametes containing $\underline{F\ \ \ L}$ or $\underline{f\ \ \ l}$ were more common than gametes containing $\underline{F\ \ \ l}$ or $\underline{f\ \ \ L}$. But how do these new combinations $\underline{F\ \ \ l}$ and $\underline{f\ \ \ L}$ arise? The answer is that, during meiosis, chromatids from homologous chromosomes exchange material in the process known as crossing over. The consequence is that an individual does not always pass on to its offspring exactly identical chromosomes to those which it received from its parents.

5.2 *Crossing over*

During interphase preceding meiosis, each chromosome replicates itself and becomes two chromatids. These are identical to each other and are called sister chromatids. During prophase I of meiosis each chromosome (a pair of sister chromatids) pairs gene for gene with its homologue. While they are closely associated, non-sister chromatids exchange segments by breaking and rejoining. This exchange of genetic material is called **crossing over**, because genes from each homologue have crossed over to the other. Figure 2 gives an outline of the genetic consequences of crossing over.

Figure 2 *Diagrammatic representation of crossing over in a heterozygote*

1 Before meiosis begins, each homologue replicates itself.

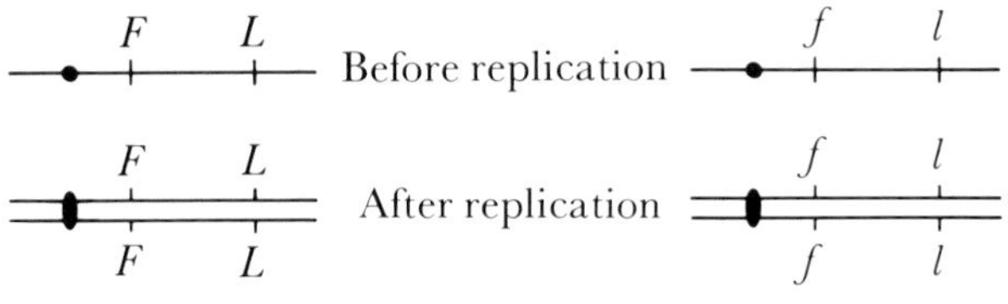

The two identical sister chromatids are connected through the centromere, represented by a dot in the diagrams.

2 In prophase I the homologues pair with each other.

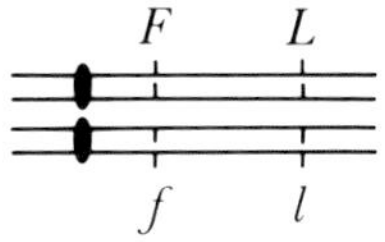

3 While they are close to each other, a chromatid may break and rejoin to a chromatid of the other homologue. The two chromatids break in exactly the same place and segments of identical size are exchanged.

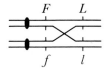

The alleles have now recombined in two of the chromatids.

4 At anaphase I the chromosomes separate.

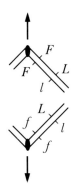

5 At anaphase II the chromatids separate.

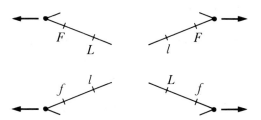

6 In this example there has been one crossover between two chromatids which results in four gamete genotypes.

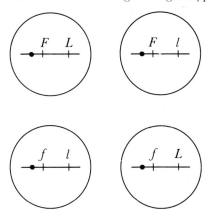

The chromosomes F L and f l are the same as the chromosomes which the F_1 plant inherited from its parents and are therefore known as **parental chromosomes, non-recombinant chromosomes** or simply **non-recombinants**. They carry the parental combination of alleles. The chromosomes F l and f L do not have the same allele combinations as those in the parental generation and are called **non-parental chromosomes**. They have been produced as a result of crossing over between the 'F' and 'L' loci in the heterozygote and so are called **crossover products**. They carry new combinations of alleles and so are also known as **recombinant chromosomes** or **recombinants**. These terms are summarized in Figure 3.

Figure 3 *Summary of terms*

Parental chromosomes

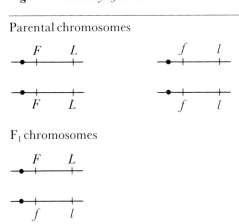

F_1 chromosomes

Chromosomes in gametes of F_1

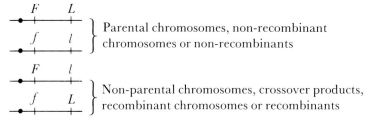

In the example used in Figure 1, a single crossover has occurred between the loci and two chromatids have been involved in exchange of material. However, either of the events in Figure 4 could also happen, and in addition to these there can be much more complicated events which need not concern us.

Remember that a very large number of cells may be undergoing meiosis in the reproductive organs of an animal or plant. In males, perhaps millions of cells are dividing in this way. Only in a proportion of these cells will crossing over occur between the loci in question. In a

Figure 4 *Possible events in prophase I*

Event	Result
No crossing over between the loci 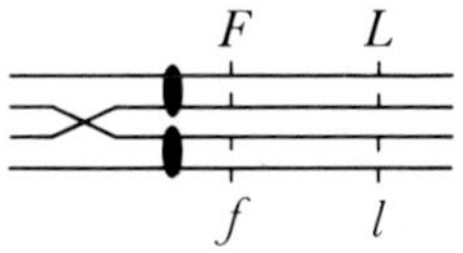	All products carry parental combinations of alleles

Event	Result
Crossing over between the loci and exchange of material in both sister chromatids in both homologues 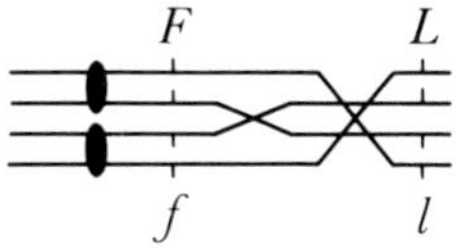	All products carry recombinant chromosomes

double heterozygote, one such crossover will produce two recombinant chromosomes, one being the opposite combination to the other. If we could detect the genotype of every gamete, we would normally expect to find equal numbers of the two types of parental combinations and equal numbers of the two types of recombinants. The number of recombinants compared with the number of non-recombinants will vary according to the loci under investigation. The proportion of gametes carrying recombinant chromosomes is related to the proximity of the gene loci. The closer they are, the lower the likelihood of crossing over between them. If they are very close then recombinants will be extremely rare. In fact the frequency of occurrence of recombinants can be used to give an estimate of the relative distances between the loci (see section 5.5).

5.2.1   What would be the recombinant chromosomes if the parental genotypes are

(a) $\dfrac{T\ \ R}{t\ \ r}$,   (b) $\dfrac{P\ \ q}{p\ \ Q}$?

5.3   *The dihybrid backcross involving linked genes*

When a double heterozygote, *Aa Bb*, is crossed with a double homozygous recessive, *aa bb*, the expected outcome is a 1 : 1 : 1 : 1 ratio *if the genes are segregating independently*. Consider first just such a cross. Table 3 gives the results of a cross between homozygous recessive black bodied, bent winged fruit flies (*b/b bt/bt*) and the double heterozygote (*B/b Bt/bt*). Notice that in Table 3 the progeny are described as having the parental or non-parental combination of traits. Here, recombination is a consequence of independent segregation. Of course, there are no corresponding recombinant chromosomes since the genes are not linked. Where there is independent segregation the expectation is that 50% of the backcross progeny have the parental combination and 50% have the non-parental combination.

Table 3 *The results of a* Drosophila *backcross*

Phenotype	Number	Genotype	Combination of traits
Normal body, normal wing	83	*B/b Bt/bt*	Parental
Black body, normal wing	82	*b/b Bt/bt*	Non-parental
Normal body, bent wing	76	*B/b bt/bt*	Non-parental
Black body, bent wing	71	*b/b bt/bt*	Parental

If, in a backcross, the outcome does not conform with the predictions of Mendel's second law, then a possible explanation is that the genes are linked. However, failure to achieve the expected ratio does not *always* indicate linkage. Mutant alleles are often associated with lower viability. This means that individuals which are homozygous for a recessive mutant allele are more likely to die before being scored and so their frequency is underestimated. Deviation from expectation due to linkage is not random. Progeny carrying either type of recombinant chromosome occur in smaller numbers than progeny carrying either type of parental chromosome. This is illustrated by the results of crosses amongst maize plants differing in two seed characters. In 'tunicate' plants, the seeds are enclosed in a green sheath (the glumes of the flower). Tunicate (T) is dominant to normal, unenclosed seeds (t). The endosperm of the seed is either starchy (S) or sugary (s). Table 4 shows the outcome of crosses between heterozygous tunicate, starchy plants and homozygous recessive non-tunicate, sugary plants.

Table 4 *Outcome of* $\dfrac{T \quad S}{t \quad s} \times \dfrac{t \quad s}{t \quad s}$

Genotype	Number	Chromosome inherited from heterozygous parent
$\dfrac{T \quad S}{t \quad s}$	326	Parental
$\dfrac{t \quad S}{t \quad s}$	111	Recombinant
$\dfrac{T \quad s}{t \quad s}$	118	Recombinant
$\dfrac{t \quad s}{t \quad s}$	295	Parental

This deficiency of recombinants is also shown in the progeny of a *Drosophila* cross. The genes for ebony body colour (*e*) and pink eye (*p*) are both recessive to their wild type alleles (*E* and *P* respectively). An ebony bodied fly was crossed to a pink eyed fly giving offspring heterozygous for both *ebony* and *pink*. The heterozygous females were then crossed to homozygous *ebony, pink* males and the backcross progeny were collected and counted. The cross and the results are shown in Table 5. Not only is there an excess of parental chromosomes in the progeny but it is apparent in both the maize and *Drosophila* data that the two types of recombinants occur in approximately equal numbers as do the two types of parentals.

Table 5 *A* Drosophila *cross involving linked genes*

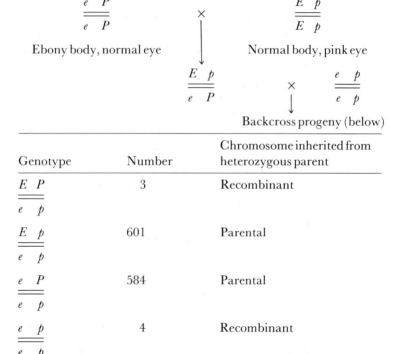

Genotype	Number	Chromosome inherited from heterozygous parent
$\frac{E\ \ P}{e\ \ p}$	3	Recombinant
$\frac{E\ \ p}{e\ \ p}$	601	Parental
$\frac{e\ \ P}{e\ \ p}$	584	Parental
$\frac{e\ \ p}{e\ \ p}$	4	Recombinant

5.3.1 Using the data in Table 3, compare numerically the effects on viability of (a) black body; (b) bent wing.

5.3.2 Use the data in Table 4. If genes 'T' and 'S' were not linked, how many of each genotype would be expected in the backcross progeny?

5.4   *The chi-square test*

Linkage between two gene loci may be suspected if a backcross does not yield a $1:1:1:1$ ratio in the progeny. However, even where genes are not linked, a *perfect* $1:1:1:1$ ratio is not necessarily obtained (see Table 3). How are we to decide whether a departure from an expected ratio is due to chance or whether it has some other cause? Small departures from a perfect ratio are expected to occur quite frequently but large departures, although possible, would occur more rarely. A statistical method called the chi-square (χ^2) test allows us to calculate the probability of observing any departure from an expected ratio. (χ is the Greek letter *chi*, pronounced like 'ki' in 'kite'). As in most statistical tests, one first has to formulate a Null Hypothesis and then the test gives the probability that the Null Hypothesis is true. For the chi-square test, the Null Hypothesis is always 'There is no difference between the observed numbers and the expected numbers.' The best way to describe the method is to work through an example.

Example 1. The data in Table 3 are assumed to fit a $1:1:1:1$ ratio. Use the chi-square test to check whether this assumption is justified.

1. First formulate the Null Hypothesis: 'There is no difference between observed numbers and expected numbers.'

2. The results of the experiment are the observed numbers. If the genes are not linked, the expected ratio is $1:1:1:1$ so the expected number in each class is

$$\frac{83 + 82 + 76 + 71}{4} = 78$$

You must always work with actual numbers of progeny, never proportions or percentages. Draw out a table of expected and observed numbers.

Genotype	*B/b Bt/bt*	*b/b Bt/bt*	*B/b bt/bt*	*b/b bt/bt*
Observed	83	82	76	71
Expected	78	78	78	78

3. For each genotype, calculate the difference between the observed and expected values $(O - E)$ and square the result $(O - E)^2$. Squaring eliminates any minus signs. Write the values of $(O - E)^2$ in the table.

4. Divide each $(O - E)^2$ by the expected value in that column. In this example it is 78 in every column, but if the expected ratio had been $9:3:3:1$ there would be different expected values in the columns. Write the $\dfrac{(O - E)^2}{E}$ values in the table, which now looks like this.

Genotype	$B/b \, Bt/bt$	$b/b \, Bt/bt$	$B/b \, bt/bt$	$b/b \, bt/bt$
Observed	83	82	76	71 *312*
Expected	78	78	78	78
$(O - E)^2$	25	16	4	49
$\dfrac{(O - E)^2}{E}$	0·321	0·205	0·051	0·628

5. Add together all the $\dfrac{(O - E)^2}{E}$ values to find the value of χ^2; $\chi^2 =$ 1·205 in this example. The formula for calculating χ^2 is therefore

$$\chi^2 = \Sigma \, \frac{(O - E)^2}{E}$$

where Σ means 'the sum of'.

6. Turn to the table of χ^2 values (Appendix). Look for a value near to your calculated value in the appropriate row of the table. The rows correspond to the 'degrees of freedom'. The number of degrees of freedom is one less than the number of items you added together to find χ^2. Our value, 1·205, falls between 1·00 and 1·42 in the 3 degrees of freedom row. Read off the probability, p, of obtaining χ^2 values as large as these from the headings of the columns. The probability of obtaining a χ^2 as high as 1·205 falls between 0·8 and 0·7.

7. The calculated χ^2 value is a measure of the deviation of the observed values from the values expected according to a theoretical (Mendelian) ratio. The deviation we have observed is expected to occur between seven and eight times in ten experiments.

8. The probability that the Null Hypothesis is true is between 0·7 and 0·8. In other words, it is quite likely that there is no difference between expected and observed numbers. We cannot say for certain that there is no difference, but by convention, we accept that any probability above 0·05 means that the Null Hypothesis is true. If the χ^2 value for 3 degrees of freedom is more than 7·82 (see χ^2 table) then p is less than 0·05 which means that there is a chance of only 5 in 100 that the observed data fit the expected ratio. We would say that there is a **significant difference** between observed and expected results. If p is greater than 0·05 then the difference between observed and expected results is **not significant**. It must be remembered that we are talking about **statistical significance**. It is up to the investigator to decide whether there is any biological significance.

Example 2. When heterozygous yellow mice were crossed amongst themselves, 1063 of the progeny were yellow and 535 were non-yellow (see problem 17). Do the data fit a $3:1$ ratio?

1. The Null Hypothesis is: 'There is no difference between the observed numbers and the numbers expected on the basis of a 3:1 ratio.'

2. Total number of progeny = 1598
   $\frac{3}{4} \times 1598 = 1198\cdot5$ and $\frac{1}{4} \times 1598 = 399\cdot5$

3, 4

	Yellow	Non-yellow
Observed	1063	535
Expected	1198·5	399·5
$(O - E)^2$	18 360	18 360
$\dfrac{(O - E)^2}{E}$	15·32	45·96

5. $\chi^2 = 61\cdot28$

6. Two items were added to obtain χ^2 so there is one degree of freedom. The calculated value is greater than 3·84, therefore the probability that the observed data fit a 3:1 ratio is less than 0·05. The Null Hypothesis is not true.

7. There is a significant difference between observed and expected results.

   In example 2, there is no question of linkage because only one locus is involved. The data do not fit a 3:1 ratio because the homozygous yellow mice die before birth. If data do not fit an expected dihybrid ratio it is not always because of linkage between the loci. A significant deviation from the expected ratio could be a result of reduced viability of one or more of the genotypes. Linkage may be suspected, however, if recombinants occur with a lower frequency than non-recombinants.

5.4.1   Use the chi-square test to find out if the data presented in Table 4 differ significantly from a 1:1:1:1 ratio.

5.4.2   Use the data in Table 3 and your answer to question 5.3.1 to calculate by the chi-square method whether the effect on viability of bent wing is statistically significant.

5.5 *Chromosome mapping*

In the *Drosophila* cross shown in Table 5, the percentage of recombinants ($\frac{7}{1192} \times 100 = 0\cdot587\%$) is much smaller than that in the maize cross shown in Table 4 ($\frac{229}{850} \times 100 = 27\%$). This means that the *ebony* and *pink* loci in *Drosophila* are very close together while *tunicate* and *sugary* in maize are much further apart. When there is independent segregation, the expected recombination frequency is 50%. If there is no linkage, 50% of the backcross progeny should be recombinants (see Table 3). If two genes are linked but are widely separated on the chromosome, they will also in effect segregate independently. Although a recombination frequency of less than 50% indicates linkage, one cannot be certain that genes which segregate independently are not linked. The loci may be the same chromosome but a long way apart.

A typical chromosome has hundreds of genes and it is possible, by the calculation of crossover frequencies between pairs of loci, to discover the order in which they lie and the relative distances between them. This is called **chromosome mapping** and one of the first chromosomes to be mapped was the X-chromosome in *Drosophila melanogaster*. When a new sex-linked eye shape mutant, *Bar* (*B*), was discovered, its relation to other sex-linked genes was worked out by the method described below.

In *Drosophila* the hook shaped Y-chromosome is represented by the symbol →. A cross was made between a bar eyed male and a white eyed female. The F₁ progeny were mated to each other and the F₂ flies were collected. The cross and the results are given in Table 6.

The number of recombinants as a percentage of the total number of progeny is 42·4%. This is called the recombination frequency (or

Table 6 *A* Drosophila *cross involving sex-linked genes*

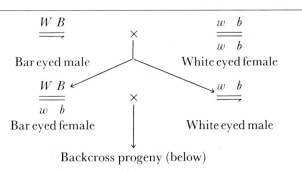

Male genotype	Number	Female genotype	Number	Phenotype	
W B →	445	*W B* / *w b*	488	Red, bar	} Parentals
w b →	375	*w b* / *w b*	426	White, normal	
W b →	383	*W b* / *w b*	332	Red, normal	} Recombinants
w B →	297	*w B* / *w b*	264	White, bar	

crossover value), and as we have seen, 50% recombination means that the genes are segregating independently. A figure of 42·4% means that the *Bar* and *white* loci are quite a long way apart.

The next part of the experiment was to find out where *Bar* lay in relation to *vermilion*, another sex-linked locus affecting eye colour, where vermilion (*v*) is recessive to its wild type allele (*V*). The crosses and results are given in Table 7.

Table 7 Drosophila *crosses with* Bar *and* vermilion

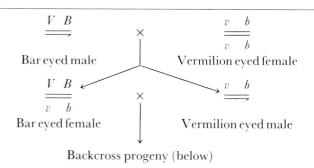

Backcross progeny (below)

Male genotype	Number	Female genotype	Number	Phenotype	
$\underrightarrow{V \quad B}$	1207	$\dfrac{V \quad B}{v \quad b}$	1353	Red, bar	Parentals
$\underrightarrow{v \quad b}$	1425	$\dfrac{v \quad b}{v \quad b}$	1487	Vermilion, normal	
$\underrightarrow{v \quad B}$	434	$\dfrac{v \quad B}{v \quad b}$	440	Vermilion, bar	Recombinants
$\underrightarrow{V \quad b}$	453	$\dfrac{V \quad b}{v \quad b}$	524	Red, normal	

The recombination frequency of *vermilion* and *Bar* is 25·3% which indicates that Bar is closer to *vermilion* than it is to *white*. But the gene loci may be arranged

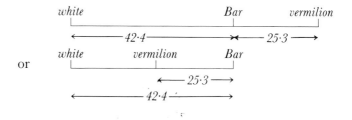

The information now required is the recombination frequency between *white* and *vermilion*. This was already known to be 30·7%. As this is less than the crossover value of *white* and *Bar*, *vermilion* must be nearer to *white* than *Bar* is to *white* so the order of the genes must be *white, vermilion, Bar*. However, the crossover frequency between *white* and *Bar* (42·4%) is less than the sum of the crossover frequencies between *white* and *vermilion* and *vermilion* and *Bar* (30·7% + 25·3% = 56%). Recombination frequencies are most likely to reflect the physical distances between loci only when they are not very far apart. This is because several crossovers involving more than two chromatids may occur between distant loci (see Figure 4). Now that about 500 gene loci have been mapped on the *Drosophila melanogaster* X-chromosome, it has become apparent that crossing over occurs more frequently in some parts of the chromosome than in others. Therefore, while recombination frequency can give an idea of the relative positions of gene loci, it does not necessarily give an accurate estimate of the real distance between them.

5.6 *The history of the chromosome theory of heredity*

What has been presented in this chapter is an explanation of linkage as it is currently understood. Such an understanding was reached by a series of observations and experiments which are outlined below in order to give the student some appreciation of the development of ideas in genetics.

When Mendel explained the results of his breeding experiments by postulating the existence of factors which segregated in the gametes and came together again in the next generation, he had no idea of what the physical nature of the factors might be. Between the publication of Mendel's paper in 1866 and its rediscovery 34 years later, great advances had been made in cytology and evidence had accumulated which led early geneticists to suspect that the chromosomes might be the carriers of the genes. Although today there is little doubt that this is the case, the 'chromosome theory of heredity' as it was called needed support from experiment.

It was known that the genes were in the nucleus because at fertilization in animals, the male transmits only the head of the sperm, the rest of the cell remaining outside the ovum. Yet the male's contribution to inheritance seemed to be equal to the female's. Even more convincing evidence that it was the chromosomes inside the nucleus which were the carriers of the genes came both from the microscopical examination of cells and from breeding experiments.

(a) The cytological evidence

(i) Constancy of chromosome number seemed to have some significance because all the somatic cells of an organism have the same number of chromosomes, as also do other members of the same sex and species. In addition, embryos which inherit abnormal chromosome numbers usually show disturbances of development.

(ii) By the time of the rediscovery of Mendel's work, the behaviour of chromosomes during gamete formation was known and it paralleled the behaviour of Mendel's factors.

(iii) If the genes maintain a constant linear order as suggested by linkage studies, then the chromosomes should retain their integrity even when they are not visible. They would not be expected to disintegrate and reform before the next cell division. The cytological evidence showed that any abnormality of chromosome structure or number was perpetuated every time the chromosomes became visible prior to successive nuclear divisions, suggesting that they do indeed remain complete.

(iv) The recombination of linked genes as demonstrated genetically also found a parallel in chromosome behaviour. Homologous chromosomes could be seen twisted around each other in cells undergoing meiosis, and later, as the chromosomes pulled apart, chromatids were visibly crossed at points called chiasmata. However, it was not possible to show that interchange of material had definitely occurred.

(b) The genetical evidence

(i) To the early geneticists the term 'linkage' did not have precisely the same meaning as described in section 5.1. What is actually observed is the inheritance of traits, not genes, and they described traits as being linked when they tended to be inherited together more frequently than expected. The first such linkage noticed was that between sex and certain other characters in *Drosophila* such as white eye and miniature wing. The existence of the sex chromosomes was known and, although their segregation followed the same pattern as the inheritance of the sex linked characters, this was no proof that the genes responsible were on the sex chromosomes. The necessary proof was to come.

(ii) The genes, it was supposed, were in a linear sequence along the chromosomes, their relative positions being related to the frequency of crossing over between them. If indeed they are in a linear order, then crossing over should exchange a number of alleles at the same time. This was shown to be the case when crossing over was investigated between three or more gene loci.

(iii) In the early years of this century an ever-increasing number of new mutant traits were being discovered in *Drosophila*. Many of these were obviously not sex linked but some showed linkage with each other. Black body colour and vestigial (very small) wings were linked to each other as also were pink eye colour and ebony body colour. However, *black* and *vestigial* segregated independently of *pink* and *ebony*. As the inheritance of more traits was worked out, they were found to be linked either to *black* and *vestigial* or to *pink* and *ebony*. These groups of linked traits or 'linkage groups' were approximately equal in size and were supposed to correspond to genes on the two pairs of large autosomes in *Drosophila melanogaster*. This species also has a very small pair of autosomes. It was not long before a new mutant trait, bent wings, was found which was linked to no other trait then known. On the basis of the chromosome theory, the gene responsible must lie on the small pair of chromosomes. A good theory is one which allows predictions to be made: the chromosome theory predicted (a) that no other genes could be discovered which would segregate independently of all those already known, and (b) that any new gene which is linked to *bent* must necessarily be close to it, therefore showing low crossover frequencies. Both of these predictions have been amply borne out in subsequent investigations. The linkage group including *bent* is small as would be expected if the genes of which it is constituted lie on the small pair of chromosomes. This correspondence between size and number of linkage groups and chromosome pairs has also been found in other species.

(iv) The critical experiment which left no doubt as to the validity of the theory was published by Bridges in 1916. By the use of **XXY** *Drosophila* females and X0 males he was able to present convincing evidence that even where the inheritance of the sex chromosomes was abnormal, the sex linked genes followed in an identical pattern. In the following year, further support came from the observation that when a piece of X-chromosome was missing, so too were all the genes which had been localized to that section by crossover studies.

Two biological disciplines, cytology and genetics, had thus been amalgamated, paving the way for the elucidation of the chemical nature of the genes and in time leading to the emergence of a new branch of biology, molecular genetics.

5.7 *Chromosome mutations*

The fusion of cytology and genetics in confirmation of the chromosome theory of heredity marked the beginning of the field of study called **cytogenetics**. Now that chromosomes were known to be the site of the genes, unusual gene sequences which were revealed by recombination studies suggested that the underlying chromosome structure was also unusual and by 1921 four types of chromosome mutations had been discovered in *Drosophila*.

Chromosome mutations affect the number of chromosomes or the number or arrangement of genes, in contrast to gene mutations (section 2.2) which affect only one or a few base pairs within a gene. Gene and chromosome mutations are distinguished by the amount of DNA involved. Both kinds occur spontaneously with a very low frequency but may be induced by ultraviolet light, ionizing radiation or chemicals such as mustard gas. Such agents, capable of bringing about mutations, are called **mutagens**.

(a) *Changes in the arrangement of genes*

In most individuals of a species, the sequence of genes on any particular chromosome is generally the same (Figure 5(i)) but a rearrangement may occur where a segment of a chromosome has an **inversion** (Figure 5(ii) and (iii)). This kind of mutation is thought to occur when a chromosome forms a tight loop and breaks in two places. The segment between the breaks untwists slightly and the ends rejoin but not in the original configuration. Another type of mutation occurs when two different, non-homologous chromosomes break and rejoin but in such a way that they exchange segments. This kind of rearrangement is called a **reciprocal translocation** (Figure 5(iv) and (v)).

An individual who possesses gene rearrangements may be unaffected phenotypically although occasionally the position of a gene in relation to other genes can affect its expression. Fertility may be reduced in organisms where two homologues carry different gene arrangements. Homologous regions will pair during prophase of meiosis and the chromosomes may have to adopt unusual configurations to make this possible. If crossing over occurs in the rearranged segment, the meiotic products will receive incomplete chromosomes and such products will not form viable gametes. Consequently, an inversion heterozygote transmits to its offspring chromosomes carrying only the parental combination of alleles in the region of the inversion.

(b) *Changes in the number of genes on chromosomes*

When there is genetic exchange between homologues during meiosis, it is normal for exactly the same amount of DNA to be exchanged. On rare occasions, unequal crossing over occurs such that one homologue gains DNA and the other loses the same amount. One chromosome has a duplicated region and the other is deficient. The mutations are called **duplication** and **deletion** (or **deficiency**) respectively (Figure 6(ii) and (iii)). If a gamete carrying a duplication or deletion is viable and fuses with a normal gamete, the individual so produced may show phenotypic

Figure 5 *Chromosome mutations involving rearrangement of genes*

(i) Original sequence of gene loci

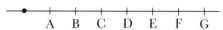

(ii) The chromosome loops and breaks occur at the overlapping region.

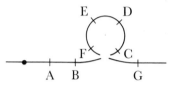

(iii) The result is an inversion.

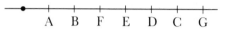

(iv) Two non-homologous chromosomes break where they overlap and then rejoin.

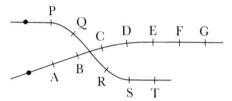

(v) The result is a reciprocal translocation.

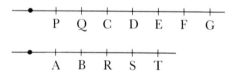

effects of the chromosome mutation. For instance, *Bar* in *Drosophila* (section 5.5) is a short duplication, and some recessive lethal 'alleles' are in fact deletions. They are lethal when homozygous because an individual who is totally lacking an essential piece of DNA is not able to synthesize vital gene products.

A second way in which deletion may arise is by chromosome breakage followed by loss of the segment which does not include the centromere. Deletions which are large enough to be recognizable under the microscope will usually have some deleterious effect on the phenotype even if the homologous chromosome is intact. A condition called cri-du-chat syndrome in humans is the result of deletion of a small part of one chromosome. Affected babies cry like a cat in distress and suffer severe mental retardation.

Instead of two homologues separating as they should during meiosis

Figure 6 *Chromosome mutations involving the number of genes on a chromosome*

(i) Original sequence of gene loci.

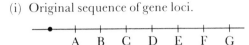

(ii) Duplication.

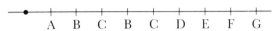

(iii) Deficiency or deletion.

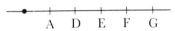

anaphase I, they may stick together and both go to the same pole of the spindle. This is called **non-disjunction** and results in one meiotic product having two copies of the chromosome and the other product having none. If the first forms a gamete which fuses with a normal gamete, the zygote will have three copies of the chromosome and is called **trisomic**. A zygote or organism which has only one copy of a chromosome instead of two is said to be **monosomic**. Monosomy in effect is a deletion of a whole chromosome and is nearly always lethal in humans. An exception is the X0 condition described in chapter 4.

Individuals with Down's syndrome are trisomic for one of the small chromosomes, number 21. A zygote with an extra chromosome 21 develops into a child with characteristic facial features, mental retardation and often congenital heart disease. Trisomy of another chromosome leads to a baby with more serious defects and a very short life expectancy, but in general, trisomy causes death of the human embryo at a very early stage of development. Again the sex chromosomes are exceptional. Extra X- or Y-chromosomes do not have such serious consequences for development as do extra autosomes.

Occasionally two non-homologous chromosomes fuse at their centromeres when these are situated at the end of the chromosome. In humans, chromosome 21 sometimes becomes attached to chromosome 14 and together they form a single chromosome. Although the total chromosome number is reduced, the cells carry a full complement of genes and so the phenotype is unaffected. However, meiosis may be irregular and unbalanced gametes are produced. Figure 7 shows the consequences of whole chromosome translocation.

Most animals have two copies of each chromosome and are therefore described as diploid (2*n*) and their gametes are haploid (*n*) but very rarely a diploid gamete is produced. If this fuses with a normal haploid gamete, the zygote has three sets of chromosomes and is said to be **triploid** (3*n*). Amongst plants, this condition is quite frequent. Meiosis

Figure 7 *Segregation in a cell carrying fused chromosomes*

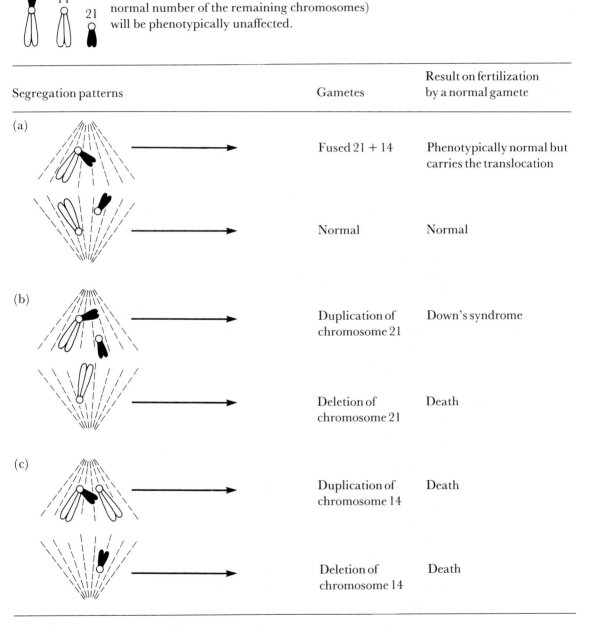

14 + 21

14
21

A person with this karyotype (plus the normal number of the remaining chromosomes) will be phenotypically unaffected.

Segregation patterns	Gametes	Result on fertilization by a normal gamete
(a)	Fused 21 + 14	Phenotypically normal but carries the translocation
	Normal	Normal
(b)	Duplication of chromosome 21	Down's syndrome
	Deletion of chromosome 21	Death
(c)	Duplication of chromosome 14	Death
	Deletion of chromosome 14	Death

is irregular in triploids because the three homologues do not segregate properly at anaphase I and the plant cannot produce viable gametes. However, triploid varieties may persist if they are able to reproduce asexually. Possession of three or more sets of chromosomes in each cell is called **polyploidy** and it is very common amongst plant species. Polyploid cells and the plants which they constitute tend to be bigger than diploids.

The chromosomes of related species are similar to each other in many respects and what differences there are can often be inferred to have arisen by one or more of the chromosome mutations described above. Chromosome mutations as well as gene mutations have played a part in the evolution of species. Currently there is much interest amongst biologists in the evolution of chromosomes themselves. The new techniques of recombinant DNA research (genetic engineering) are revealing hitherto unknown gene structures and are stimulating exciting ideas about biological adaptation and evolutionary processes.

5.7.1 By 1926 a map of part of the third chromosome of *Drosophila melanogaster* had been worked out and the order of the genes is shown in the diagram.

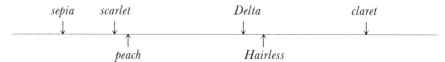

Corresponding genes also occur in the closely related species *D. simulans* and recombination data were collected for this species to discover whether the gene loci were similarly arranged. The results are shown in the table.

Gene loci	Recombination frequency (%)
sepia – scarlet	27
Delta – scarlet	28
Hairless – Delta	2
scarlet – Hairless	17
Delta – peach	35
peach – claret	29
Delta – claret	45

(a) The *sepia* and *claret* loci are situated at each end of the region as in *D. melanogaster*. Use the recombination data to work out the order of the other gene loci on the *D. simulans* chromosome. (Hint: draw a line with *sepia* at the left-hand side. Take the data in the order given and use a ruler to plot the relative positions of the gene loci.)

(b) Explain the difference in the order in terms of chromosome mutation.

5.7.2 Figure 8 shows human chromosomes as they appear in mitosis. What would be the phenotype of a person with this karyotype? (The easiest way to discover the karyotype is to prepare a karyogram as described in the caption to Figure 1 of chapter 4. You may photocopy Figure 8.)

Figure 8 *Human chromosomes in mitosis*

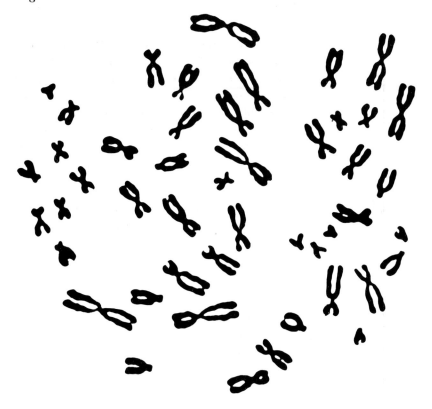

5.8 Summary

Gene loci are said to be linked when they are on the same pair of homologous chromosomes. When two loci are closely linked, the segregation of one pair of alleles is not independent of the segregation of the other pair and the characteristic $9:3:3:1$ and $1:1:1:1$ dihybrid ratios are not obtained. A statistical method called the chi-square (χ^2) test can be used to check whether a discrepancy between results expected on the basis of a Mendelian ratio and results actually obtained, could be due to chance, or whether it is so unusual as to make a biological explanation more likely.

In a double heterozygote, the two dominant genes may be on one homologue and the two recessive genes on the other, or each homologue may carry one dominant and one recessive gene. New combinations of alleles on a chromosome occur because of crossing over between the loci during prophase of meiosis. When this happens, the new combinations are called recombinant chromosomes and those which have not recombined are called parental or non-recombinant chromosomes. A back-cross to the double homozygous recessive is normally done in order to determine which individuals carry recombinant or parental chromosomes.

Because crossing over is less likely to occur between close than between distant loci, it is possible to estimate the relative position of genes on chromosomes on the basis of the frequency of crossing over between them. This is known as chromosome mapping and the method was instrumental in establishing the fact that genes are indeed located on the chromosomes. Further evidence for the chromosome theory of heredity may be summarized under two headings.

Cytological evidence

(i) Chromosome numbers are constant within a species.

(ii) The behaviour of chromosomes at gamete formation and fertilization parallels the segregation and reunion of Mendel's factors.

(iii) The chromosomes maintain their integrity in interphase.

(iv) Crossing over in the genetical sense is paralleled by chiasmata formation at meiosis.

Genetical evidence

(i) The inheritance of sex linked characters follows the same pattern as the inheritance of the sex chromosomes to such an extent that their abnormal inheritance is identical.

(ii) Crossing over involves the exchange of groups of genes.

(iii) The number of linkage groups is the same as the number of chromosome pairs and the relative sizes of linkage groups correspond to the relative physical sizes of chromosomes.

(iv) When a piece of a chromosome is missing, so too are a number of specific genes.

Once it was established that the genes were on the chromosomes, it became apparent, through genetical experiments, that some individuals possessed rare gene arrangements. These and other chromosome mutations were confirmed by cytological studies. Chromosome mutations affect the arrangement or number of genes on a chromosome (inversions, translocations, deletions and duplications), the number of chromosomes (trisomy, monosomy and chromosome fusion) or the number of sets of chromosomes (polyploidy). The effect of a chromosome mutation on the phenotype of the organism which carries it ranges from zero to lethal and fertility is often reduced in viable individuals.

Chromosomes themselves evolve and chromosome mutations are an important factor in the evolution of species.

Key words

	Section		Section
chi-square (χ^2)	5.4	mutagen	5.7
chromosome mapping	5.5	non-disjunction	5.7
crossing over	5.2	non-parental chromosome	5.2
crossover products	5.2	non-recombinant	
cytogenetics	5.7	chromosome	5.2
deficiency	5.7	parental chromosome	5.2
deletion	5.7	polyploidy	5.7
duplication	5.7	recombinant chromosome	5.2
inversion	5.7	statistical significance	5.4
linked genes	5.1	translocation	5.7
monosomic	5.7	triploid	5.7
		trisomic	5.7

Answers

5.2.1   (a) $\underline{T \quad r}$ and $\underline{t \quad R}$;   (b) $\underline{P \quad Q}$ and $\underline{p \quad q}$.

5.3.1   Total number of flies = 312, of which half should be black body and half should be bent wing.
    (a) 153 are black so *black* does not appear to reduce viability.
    (b) 147 have bent wings so *bent* does not appreciably reduce viability either.

5.3.2   There are 850 seeds altogether and if 'T' and 'S' are not linked, the four genotypes should appear in a $1:1:1:1$ ratio in the backcross progeny. $212·5$ seeds are expected in each genotype group.

5.4.1   The expected number in each of the four groups is $212·5$ (question 5.3.2)
$$\chi^2 = 60·62 + 48·48 + 42·02 + 32·03$$
$$= 183·15$$
With 3 degrees of freedom, $p < 0·001$ which means that the observed data are significantly different from numbers expected on the basis of a $1:1:1:1$ ratio.

5.4.2   156 flies are expected to have normal wings and 156 are expected to have bent wings (see question 5.3.1).
$$\chi^2 = 0·519 + 0·519$$
$$= 1·04$$
With one degree of freedom, $p > 0·3$. There is no significant difference between observed and expected values.

5.7.1   (a) The order is *sepia, scarlet, Hairless, Delta, peach, claret*.
    (b) *Hairless, Delta* and *peach* are inverted in comparison with *D. melanogaster*, so the mutation is an inversion. It is not possible from the information given to say which is the original sequence.

5.7.2   A male with Down's syndrome.

PROBLEMS

51 In budgerigars, a gene locus for feather colour is linked to a locus controlling the intensity of colour (see also problem 31). The following table gives the possible genotypes and their corresponding phenotypes.

		Intensity locus		
		i^1i^1	i^1i^2	i^2i^2
colour	*BB* or *Bb*	Light green	Dark green	Olive
locus	*bb*	Sky blue	Cobalt	Mauve

(a) An olive bird ($BB\,i^2i^2$) is crossed to a sky blue bird. What will be the phenotype and genotype of the F_1 progeny?

(b) F_1 birds from the cross above are backcrossed to sky blue birds. What are the possible phenotypes of the progeny assuming that crossing over can occur?

(c) As the genes are linked, which phenotypes will be most frequent in the backcross progeny?

52 *Cosmos bipinnatus* is a member of the daisy family (*Compositae*). One pair of alleles gives either crimson flower colour (*P*) or pink flower colour (*p*). Another pair of alleles gives either flat petals (*I*) or inrolled petals (*i*). Plants with the genotype *Pp Ii* were backcrossed to plants with the genotype *pp ii*. The results are given in the table below.

Cross no.	Crimson		Pink		Total
	Inrolled	Flat	Inrolled	Flat	
1	63	5	4	102	174
2	12	1	0	7	20
3	13	2	1	9	25
4	21	1	2	18	42
5	7	1	0	8	16
Total	116	10	7	144	277

How do these data indicate linkage between the 'P' and 'I' loci?

53 In *Drosophila*, the mutant genes *eyeless* (*ey*) and *cubitus interruptus* (*ci*) are recessive to their wild type alleles, *Ey* and *Ci* respectively. The two gene loci are situated very close to each other on the same chromosome. The eyes are absent or nearly so in *eyeless* homozygotes, and *cubitus interruptus* affects the presence of a wing vein. If a fly with the genotype $\dfrac{ci\quad ey}{ci\quad ey}$ is crossed to a wild type fly, the F_1 will be $\dfrac{Ci\quad Ey}{ci\quad ey}$. If there is no crossing over between the loci, what will be the phenotypic ratio in the F_2?

54 Read the information about *eyeless* and *cubitus interruptus* in problem 53. An eyeless *Drosophila*, homozygous for the wild type allele affecting the wing vein character, is crossed to a cubitus interruptus fly which is homozygous for the wild type allele affecting the eye character.

(a) Using the symbolism for linked genes, give the genotype of the F_1.

(b) If there is no crossing over between the loci, what will be the phenotypic ratio in the F_2?

55 The nail–patella syndrome is a condition in humans where the knee-cap fails to develop and the fingernails are small. It is due to a dominant gene and is unknown in the homozygous condition. The gene locus is on the same chromosome as the locus controlling the ABO blood groups. In the following pedigree, the shaded symbols represent persons with the nail–patella syndrome. Genotypes for blood groups are indicated.

What is the most likely blood group of child X? Show your reasoning.

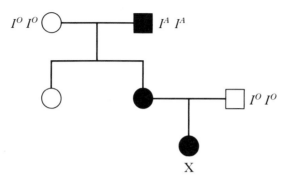

56 Ten week stocks are available in two varieties, single and double. In the double forms, the stamens are replaced by petals. The flowers are sterile and so it is impossible to breed from them. Doubling is due to a recessive allele, *s*. A dominant allele, *G*, at another gene locus makes the cotyledons and leaves of the seedlings pale green instead of the normal dark green. A gardener bought a packet of seed and was instructed that if he pulled out and destroyed all the pale green seedlings, he would be left with only double flowered plants.

(a) With respect to the 'S' locus only, give the genotypes of the parents of the seed in the packet.

(b) What proportion of the seeds would become double flowered stocks?

(c) The parents of the seeds are heterozygous at the 'G' locus. When the seeds germinate, what proportion of the seedlings will be dark green?

(d) Assuming that the 'S' and 'G' loci segregate independently, what proportion of the dark green seedlings should develop double flowers?

(e) Using appropriate symbols, explain how it is that all the dark green seedlings develop double flowers.

57   A mutant *Drosophila* called 'bifid wing' was discovered in 1912. The gene responsible, *bf*, is recessive and sex linked. Bifid winged males with wild type eye colour, genotype $\overrightarrow{bf\ V}$, were crossed with females heterozygous for *bifid* and *vermilion* (eye colour), genotype $\dfrac{bf\ V}{Bf\ v}$. The male progeny of this cross were collected and counted and the results are given below.

Phenotype of male	Number
Wild type wings, vermilion eyes	57
Bifid wings, wild type eyes	85
Wild type wings and eye colour	31
Bifid wings, vermilion eyes	33

(a) Give the genotypes of the four kinds of male progeny ($\longrightarrow$ represents the *Drosophila* Y-chromosome).

(b) Which are the crossover classes?

58   In rats, cinnamon coat colour is recessive to grey and curly coat is dominant to straight. Cinnamon, straight haired females (*b/b cu/cu*) were mated to grey, curly males (*B/B Cu/Cu*). The F_1 animals were grey and curly and were backcrossed to animals with their mother's genotype. The following results were obtained.

Phenotype	Number
Grey, curly	190
Grey, straight	125
Cinnamon, curly	128
Cinnamon, straight	182

(a) Give the phenotypes and genotypes of the recombinant classes.

(b) What would be the expected numbers in each class if the genes for coat colour and hair type are segregating independently?

(c) Use the chi-square method to detect whether the difference between expected and observed numbers is statistically significant.

(d) Give the genotypes of all the classes in the backcross progeny using the most appropriate method.

59 King and Castle discovered that in rats, *albino* and *waltzer* are linked. Both mutant alleles are recessive to wild type. In a backcross, the following progeny were obtained.

Phenotype	Number
Albino, non-waltzer	146
Albino, waltzer	38
Coloured, non-waltzer	37
Coloured, waltzer	159

(a) Define gene symbols and, using the conventional method of showing linked genes, give the genotypes of the parents of the backcross progeny.

(b) If the genes were not linked, how many backcross progeny would be expected in each phenotypic class?

60 Albino mice (*cc*) have no pigment and so have no colouring in their fur or eyes. The eyes appear pink because blood can be seen in the vessels. A recessive allele, *p*, at another gene locus also produces pink eyes and has a diluting effect on coloured fur, making it appear paler. Albino mice (*cc PP*) were crossed with dilute coloured, pink eyed mice (*CC pp*) and produced a total of 142 F_1 progeny, all coloured and dark eyed. These were crossed amongst themselves and had a total of 580 F_2 young in the following phenotypic classes.

Phenotype	Number
Dark eyed, coloured	295
Pink eyed, dilute coloured	129
Albino	156

(a) Give the expected number in the three phenotypic classes in the F_2 progeny:
   (i) if the loci were segregating independently;
   (ii) if the genes were linked and were so close that no crossing over occurred between them.

(b) What evidence is there for linkage between *albino* and *pink*?

(c) What is the word used to describe an allele like *pink* which affects more than one character?

61 Recombination experiments have allowed the construction of linkage maps for the chromosomes of many diploid species but, of these, perhaps least is known about linkage in humans. Why do you think this is so?

62 Demerec crossed two pure breeding maize plants. One was normal size and grown from a seed with shrunken endosperm (genotype *D/D sh/sh*) and the other was dwarf and grown from a seed with normal endosperm (genotype *d/d Sh/Sh*). The F_1 seeds had normal endosperm and grew into normal sized plants. The F_1 plants were allowed to self fertilize and the F_2 progeny fell into the following classes.

Phenotype	Number
Normal endosperm, normal size	329
Normal endosperm, dwarf	162
Shrunken endosperm, normal size	138
Shrunken endosperm, dwarf	8

(a) What would be the expected numbers in each phenotypic class if the genes for endosperm type and plant size were segregating independently?

(b) Use the chi-square method to discover whether the deviation from expected is statistically significant.

(c) Assuming that the different classes are equally viable, give a full explanation for the differences between observed and expected numbers. (Hint: use a Punnett square to discover which genotypes are occurring with a greater than expected frequency.)

63 In an early experiment on linkage in *Drosophila*, Dexter crossed yellow bodied, white eyed males with wild type females and obtained all wild type F_1 progeny. These were allowed to interbreed and 11 394 F_2 progeny were collected. 6081 of the F_2 generation were female and wild type for both eye colour and body colour. The F_2 males fell into the four phenotypic classes shown below.

Phenotype of F_2 males	Number
Wild type body and eye colour	2870
Yellow body, wild type eye	34
Wild type body, white eye	36
Yellow body, white eye	2373

(a) What evidence is there, in the above information, that *white* and *yellow* are both on the X-chromosome?

(b) The genotype of a yellow bodied, white eyed male is represented $\underset{\Longrightarrow}{y\ \ w}$ where $\longrightarrow$ represents the Y-chromosome. Show in a similar manner the genotypes of the other three classes of males.

(c) (i)   What is the ratio of wild type to yellow in the F_2 males?
     (ii) What is the expected ratio?
     (iii) The difference is statistically significant. How can you account for it?

(d) Dexter then did the following cross:

$$\frac{Y \quad w}{y \quad W} \times \frac{y \quad w}{=\!=\!=} \longrightarrow$$

    (i) What are the phenotypes of these flies?

    (ii) What are the phenotypes of their male progeny?

    (iii) Which will be the rarest phenotypic classes in the male progeny?

64 Three linked gene loci in the rabbit are:

    (1) 'C', coat colour: agouti (C), himalayan (c^h), chinchilla (c^{ch}), albino (c).

    (2) 'B', coat colour: black (B) and brown (b). Black and brown are only expressed in the absence of C or cc.

    (3) 'Y', fat colour: white (Y) and yellow (y).

Castle crossed brown, chinchilla, yellow fat animals ($c^{ch}c^{ch}\ bb\ yy$) with black, himalayan, white fat animals ($c^hc^h\ BB\ YY$). The F_1 progeny were backcrossed to $cc\ bb\ yy$ and a total of 908 progeny were obtained which fell into the eight classes given below.

Genotype	Number	Genotype	Number
$c^hc\ Bb\ Yy$	276	$c^{ch}c\ Bb\ Yy$	55
$c^hc\ Bb\ yy$	7	$c^{ch}c\ Bb\ yy$	108
$c^hc\ bb\ Yy$	125	$c^{ch}c\ bb\ Yy$	16
$c^hc\ bb\ yy$	46	$c^{ch}c\ bb\ yy$	275

(a) Using the symbolism for linked genes, give the genotype of the F_1 heterozygotes. (The order of the genes does not matter.)

(b) Write out each of the eight genotypes in the backcross progeny in a similar manner.

(c) Which of the classes in the backcross progeny have inherited parental chromosomes from the heterozygous parent?

(d) How many of the 908 progeny carry a crossover product between:

    (i) 'Y' and 'B';   (ii) 'Y' and 'C';   (iii) 'C' and 'B'?

(e) Which are the two closest loci?

(f) Which is the middle locus?

(g) Which two classes of genotypes in the backcross progeny are the result of two crossovers, one each side of the middle gene?

65 Altenberg investigated linkage relationships between three gene loci in *Primula sinensis*:

    (1) 'L', length of style: short style (L) and long style (l).

    (2) 'R', flower colour: magenta (R) and red (r).

    (3) 'S', stigma colour: green (S) and red (s).

He backcrossed $\dfrac{l \quad r \quad s}{L \quad R \quad S}$ to $\dfrac{l \quad r \quad s}{l \quad r \quad s}$. The order given in the genotypes is the order of the gene loci on the chromosome. The genotypes and numbers of the backcross progeny were as follows:

Genotype	Number	Genotype	Number
$\dfrac{l \quad r \quad s}{l \quad r \quad s}$	1032	$\dfrac{L \quad R \quad S}{l \quad r \quad s}$	1063
$\dfrac{L \quad r \quad s}{l \quad r \quad s}$	156	$\dfrac{l \quad R \quad S}{l \quad r \quad s}$	180
$\dfrac{l \quad R \quad s}{l \quad r \quad s}$	54	$\dfrac{L \quad r \quad S}{l \quad r \quad s}$	39
$\dfrac{l \quad r \quad S}{l \quad r \quad s}$	526	$\dfrac{L \quad R \quad s}{l \quad r \quad s}$	634

(a) Which genotypes carry only parental chromosomes?
(b) Calculate the frequency of crossing over between 'L' and 'R'.
(c) Calculate the frequency of crossing over between 'R' and 'S'.
(d) Which genotypes carry chromosomes which can only be the result of double crossing over?

6 Population genetics

6.1 Genes in populations and the Hardy–Weinberg equation

We have seen how Mendelian genetic analysis can be used to calculate the expected proportions of different genotypes and phenotypes in the progeny of two parents whose genotypes are known. Exactly the same principles can be applied when the progeny come not from just one pair of parents but from a large number of interbreeding individuals. The method used to calculate the expected proportions of different genotypes in a population was published in 1908 by the British mathematician G. H. Hardy and, independently, by the German physician W. Weinberg. It is now known as the Hardy–Weinberg equation and its derivation will be described in easy stages.

If we cross a single pair of parents, both heterozygous Aa, the proportion of genotypes in their progeny can be calculated using a Punnett square (Table 1). The probabilities of the zygotes are calculated as the product of the frequencies of gametes involved in their formation. In a monohybrid cross between heterozygotes, the two types of gametes occur in equal proportions.

Table 1 *Punnett square showing progeny of two heterozygotes*

		Gametes from male	
		$\frac{1}{2}A$	$\frac{1}{2}a$
Gametes from females	$\frac{1}{2}A$	$\frac{1}{4}AA$	$\frac{1}{4}Aa$
	$\frac{1}{2}a$	$\frac{1}{4}Aa$	$\frac{1}{4}aa$

Now consider a situation where there are two males and two females which breed at random with each other. The females are genotypes AA and Aa. The males are also genotypes AA and Aa. Both genotypes produce the same number of gametes but while Aa produces half of each kind, AA produces all A. Therefore $\frac{3}{4}$ of all the gametes are A and $\frac{1}{4}$ are a. The males and females breed at random and the probabilities of the three possible genotypes in their progeny are obtained as before. The outcome is shown in Table 2.

Table 2 *Outcome of a cross where $\frac{3}{4}$ of gametes carry A and $\frac{1}{4}$ carry a*

		Gametes from males			
		$\frac{1}{4}A$	$\frac{1}{4}A$	$\frac{1}{4}A$	$\frac{1}{4}a$
Gametes from females	$\frac{1}{4}A$ $\frac{1}{4}A$ $\frac{1}{4}A$	$\frac{9}{16} = 0{\cdot}5625\,AA$			$\frac{3}{16} = 0{\cdot}1875\,Aa$
	$\frac{1}{4}a$	$\frac{3}{16} = 0{\cdot}1875\,Aa$			$\frac{1}{16} = 0{\cdot}0625\,aa$

Next consider an indeterminate number of males and females breeding at random. We do not need to know what their genotypes are. All we need is the proportion or frequency of the two types of gametes. As in Table 2, the frequency of allele A is $0{\cdot}75$ and of allele a, $0{\cdot}25$. The probabilities of the three types of zygote are shown in Table 3. If the frequencies of the alleles are represented by p and q, the table can be simplified (Table 4). You will see that the probabilities of the zygotes are given by the equation $(p + q)^2 = 1$, where 1 means the whole population. Expanded, this becomes

$$p^2 + 2pq + q^2 = 1$$

which is the **Hardy–Weinberg equation**.

Table 3 *Outcome of a cross where frequency of A is 0·75 and frequency of a is 0·25*

		Gametes from males	
		$0{\cdot}75\,A$	$0.25\,a$
Gametes from females	$0{\cdot}75\,A$	$0{\cdot}75^2 = 0{\cdot}5625\,AA$	$0{\cdot}75 \times 0{\cdot}25 = 0{\cdot}1875\,Aa$
	$0{\cdot}25\,a$	$0{\cdot}75 \times 0{\cdot}25 = 0{\cdot}1875\,Aa$	$0{\cdot}25^2 = 0.0625\,aa$

Table 4 *The probabilities of zygotes from union of gametes with frequencies p and q*

		Gametes from males	
		$p\,(A)$	$q\,(a)$
Gametes from females	$p\,(A)$	$p^2\,(AA)$	$pq\,(Aa)$
	$q\,(a)$	$pq\,(Aa)$	$q^2\,(aa)$

A population to which the Hardy–Weinberg equation is applicable consists of diploid, sexually reproducing individuals. Mating should be random with respect to the gene locus in question and this is most likely to be the case when the population is large. The members of the population can be imagined as contributing equally to a 'pool' of gametes in which pairs fuse to form the zygotes of the next generation. To get an idea of the random union of gametes, imagine an externally fertilizing animal such as the cod where both males and females release millions of gametes into the sea. What is of interest is the genes in those gametes. The sum total of genes in the gametes of a population is known as the **gene pool**. The gene pool consists of all the genes at every locus which can be passed on to the next generation. A population consists of all those individuals which share in a common gene pool. In population genetics we are concerned with only one gene locus which has two alleles. In the gene pool of say 1000 individuals, this gene locus is represented 2000 times. A certain proportion (p) of these 2000 genes are one allele (A) and the rest (q) are the other allele (a). p and q must be expressed either as fractions or as decimals and they must add up to 1.

Before pursuing some applications of the Hardy–Weinberg equation, the meaning of the terms is summarized below.

Summary of the meaning of the terms in the Hardy–Weinberg equation

p^2 = frequency of one homozygote (AA)
$2pq$ = frequency of the heterozygote (Aa)
q^2 = frequency of the other homozygote (aa)

where

p = frequency of one of the alleles (A)
q = frequency of the other allele (a)

There are only two alleles so

$$p + q = 1$$

Note that p^2, $2pq$ and q^2 are genotype frequencies while p and q are allele frequencies.

6.2 *Applications of the Hardy–Weinberg equation*

If we know the frequency of one of the alleles in a gene pool, we can use the equation to calculate the expected proportions of genotypes in the population.

Example 1. Calculation of genotype frequencies given allele frequencies. A breeding population of *Drosophila* is maintained in a large container in a laboratory. The frequency of the allele for black body (*b*) in this population is 0·3 and the frequency of the normal allele (*B*) is 0·7. What are the expected proportions of the genotypes *BB*, *Bb* and *bb*?

The frequency of $b = 0.3 = q$
The frequency of $B = 0.7 = p$

(The recessive allele is normally assigned the frequency q but there is no rule governing this. It does not matter whether it is p or q as long as the terms in the equation correspond with the appropriate genotypes.)

Using the Hardy–Weinberg equation, $p^2 + 2pq + q^2 = 1$,

frequency of genotype $BB = p^2 = 0.7^2$ $= 0.49$
frequency of genotype $Bb = 2pq = 2 \times 0.7 \times 0.3 = 0.42$
frequency of genotype $bb = q^2 = 0.3^2$ $= 0.09$
                                      Total   1·00

The experimenter would know that the frequency of the allele for black was 0·3 because he would have started the population with say 100 pairs of flies of which 30 pairs would be black. The black and wild type flies would mate at random and the next generation would be expected to consist of the genotypes *BB*, *Bb* and *bb* in the proportions calculated above.

In natural populations, allele frequencies are normally calculated from observed genotype frequencies. This may seem like circular reasoning because allele frequencies are then used to calculate genotype frequencies according to the equation. Notice, though, that *observed* genotype frequencies are used for the calculation of allele frequencies while the Hardy–Weinberg equation gives *expected* genotype frequencies. Observed and expected frequencies are not necessarily the same. In order to calculate allele frequencies we need to know how many individuals there are with each genotype. When one allele is completely dominant, it is usually not possible to distinguish phenotypically between homozygous dominants and heterozygotes. The situation is made easier if the alleles are codominant.

Example 2. Calculation of allele frequencies given genotype frequencies. In humans, the MN blood group system is controlled by two codominant alleles, L^M and L^N. The blood group M is genotype $L^M L^M$, group MN is genotype $L^M L^N$ and group N is genotype $L^N L^N$.

In a study of 747 Icelanders, 233 were blood group M, 385 were MN and 129 were N. What are the frequencies of alleles L^M and L^N?

Each $L^M L^M$ person contributes twice as many L^M alleles to the gene pool as an $L^M L^N$ person because all the gametes from the first genotype carry L^M but only half the gametes from the heterozygote carry this allele. Think of this in another way; each $L^M L^M$ person contributes two L^M alleles while each $L^M L^N$ person contributes one.

Total number of L^M alleles = $385 + (2 \times 233) = 851$
Total number of L^N alleles = $385 + (2 \times 129) = 643$
Total number of alleles of both kinds = $851 + 643$ (or 2×747) = 1494

$$\text{Proportion of } L^M = \frac{851}{1494} = 0.57$$

$$\text{Proportion of } L^N = \frac{643}{1494} = 0.43$$

(Although the proportion of L^N could be calculated as 1 minus the proportion of L^M, this is not recommended. It is better to calculate both values by the method shown and then to check that they sum to unity.)

6.3 The Hardy–Weinberg equilibrium

A population in which the observed genotype frequencies are the same as those expected according to the predictions of the Hardy–Weinberg equation is said to be in **Hardy–Weinberg equilibrium**.

Example 3. Comparison of observed with expected genotype frequencies. In a sample of 1279 English people, 363 were found to have the blood group M, 634 had group MN and 282 had group N. Is this population in Hardy–Weinberg equilibrium?

First calculate allele frequencies as in example 2.

Total number of alleles = $1279 \times 2 = 2558$
Total number of L^M alleles = $(2 \times 363) + 634 = 1360$
Total number of L^N alleles = $(2 \times 282) + 634 = 1198$

$$\text{Frequency of } L^M = \frac{1360}{2558} = 0.53$$

$$\text{Frequency of } L^N = \frac{1198}{2558} = 0.47$$

Let frequency of L^M = p = 0.53. Let frequency of L^N = q = 0.47. Substitute p and q in the Hardy–Weinberg equation, $p^2 + 2pq + q^2 = 1$.

$p^2 = 0.53^2 = 0.28$ = frequency of $L^M L^M$
$2pq = 2 \times 0.53 \times 0.47 = 0.50$ = frequency of $L^M L^N$
$q^2 = 0.47^2 = 0.22$ = frequency of $L^N L^N$

(Check that $p^2 + 2pq + q^2 = 1$.)

Expected number of $L^M L^M$ in population of 1279 = 1279 × 0·28 = 358
Expected number of $L^M L^N$ = 1279 × 0·50 = 640
Expected number of $L^N L^N$ = 1279 × 0·22 = 281

The observed and expected values are very close so the population is in Hardy–Weinberg equilibrium. (The difference between the actual and expected numbers can be tested for significance using the chi-square test. Although there are three genotypes, there is only one degree of freedom because we only need to know one allele frequency before all three genotype frequencies can be calculated.)

If it can be assumed from the information given that a population is in equilibrium, it is possible to calculate the other genotype frequencies knowing only the frequency of one of the homozygotes (example 4). A common error is to make the unwarranted assumption of equilibrium. If sufficient information is given then do the calculations as in examples 2 and 3.

Example 4. Calculation of other genotype frequencies given the frequency of one of the homozygotes. Albinism, the complete lack of pigment, is determined in humans by a recessive allele. The frequency of albinos in Britain is about one in 20 000 births. What proportion of the population is heterozygous for this condition?

We must assume that the population is in Hardy–Weinberg equilibrium as there is insufficient information to calculate allele frequencies in any other way. Let the allele for albinism be *a* and the normal allele be *A*.
In the Hardy–Weinberg equation, $p^2 + 2pq + q^2 = 1$,

p^2 = frequency of *AA*
$2pq$ = frequency of *Aa*
q^2 = frequency of *aa* whose frequency is given as 1 in 20 000

$$q^2 = \frac{1}{20\,000} = 0·000\,05$$

Therefore $q = \sqrt{0·000\,05} = 0·007$
$p = 1 - q = 0·993$
Frequency of heterozygotes = 2 × 0·993 × 0·007 = 0·014

Example 4 draws our attention to an important fact. Although there may be very few people in a population who are homozygous for a particular recessive allele, the proportion of heterozygotes for that allele may be quite high. In Britain 14 in 1000 are heterozygous for albinism.

6.4 *Disturbances of the Hardy–Weinberg equilibrium*

Populations are not always in equilibrium and the reasons for this are two; either the Hardy–Weinberg equation is not applicable to the population, or allele frequencies are not constant from one generation to the next.

The equation is only applicable to large, randomly mating populations of sexually reproducing diploids. If any of these conditions are not met, then the Hardy–Weinberg equation cannot predict genotype frequencies. The population, and the sample chosen from it for study, must be large enough to minimize the effects of fortuitous irregularities. Allele frequencies are likely to fluctuate in small populations because of the relatively large contribution of each individual to the gene pool. Such fluctuations are known as **genetic drift**.

Non-random mating is fairly common. While many hermaphrodite plants have some mechanism for promoting cross fertilization, others are habitually self fertilizing. This habit of inbreeding tends to increase the proportion of homozygotes at the expense of heterozygotes. The lesser snow goose of the Canadian Arctic provides another example of non-random mating. This species is usually white but there is a blue form which is determined by a single dominant autosomal gene. There is evidence that blue geese tend to choose blue mates. While non-random mating alters genotype frequencies, it does not have the same effect on allele frequencies.

6.4.1 (a) A plant with the genotype *Aa* is self fertilizing. If it has 40 F_1 progeny, how many are expected to have the genotypes *AA*, *Aa* and *aa*?
(b) What are the frequencies of alleles *A* and *a* in the F_1 generation?
(c) Each of the 40 F_1 progeny is also self fertilizing and each has 40 progeny. Out of the 1600 F_2 plants, how many will be homozygous?
(d) What are the frequencies of alleles *A* and *a* in the F_2 generation?
(e) Is the F_2 generation in Hardy–Weinberg equilibrium?

Allele frequencies may change for one or more of the following reasons.
(1) Genetic drift (see above).
(2) Mutation. Allele *A* mutates to allele *a* more often than *a* mutates to *A* or *vice versa*.
(3) Migration. Individuals move into or out of a population non-randomly with respect to a given locus.
(4) Differential reproduction. One genotype is less likely to reproduce than another.

Mutation rates are generally very low and a change in allele frequencies due to mutation would be hardly noticeable. In some cases, migration may be an important factor, especially where the number of migrants is large in comparison to the size of the population.

Differential reproduction is the most interesting factor affecting allele frequencies because by its action, alleles favourable to reproduction will increase in frequency at the expense of alternative alleles. Difference in the reproductive success of the various genotypes is brought about by **selection**. Selection means that certain individuals make a greater contribution to the gene pool than others. If the selection is the conscious choice of man then it is called **artificial selection**. If it is due to the natural circumstances of the environment it is called **natural selection**. If selective advantage is due to possession of a particular allele then the frequency of this allele will increase. Any change in allele frequencies is an evolutionary change, whatever its cause. Genetic drift, mutation and migration bring about random changes but natural selection might be expected to lead to improvements in the adaptation of organisms to their environment.

Example 5. A change in allele frequency due to differential reproduction. Thalassaemia is a disease of humans and is caused by a recessive allele. The recessive homozygote suffers from severe anaemia and usually dies before reproductive age. The heterozygote has very mild anaemia which has no effect on reproduction. In some Sardinian villages the frequency of the allele for thalassaemia (*th*) is 10%. The allele is present at such a high frequency because it is associated with resistance to malaria which until recent times was prevalent on the island.

(a) If the population is in Hardy–Weinberg equilibrium, what would be the incidence of thalassaemia at birth?

(b) If heterozygotes are at no disadvantage compared with homozygous dominants but homozygous *th/th* die before reproducing, what will be the frequency of the *th* allele in the next generation?

(a) The frequency of *th* = 10% = 0·1 = q. In the Hardy–Weinberg equation, $p^2 + 2pq + q^2 = 1$, q^2 = frequency of *th/th*

$$q^2 = 0·1^2 = 0·01$$

Therefore the incidence of thalassaemia at birth is 0·01 = 1%.

(b) q = 0·1 (given), p + q = 1, therefore p = 1 − q = 0·9. In the Hardy–Weinberg equation,

$$p^2 = \text{frequency of } Th/Th = 0·81$$
$$2pq = \text{frequency of } Th/th = 0·18$$
$$q^2 = \text{frequency of } th/th = 0·01$$

Let there be 100 in the population. (When no population size is given, it is a good idea to work from an arbitrary one.) 81 will be *Th/Th*, 18 will be *Th/th* and 1 will die from thalassaemia. The 81 *Th/Th* contribute 2 × 81 = 162 *Th* alleles to the gene pool. The 18 *Th/th* contribute 18 *Th* and 18 *th* alleles to the gene pool.

Total number of *Th* alleles = 162 + 18 = 180
Total number of *th* alleles $\qquad$ = 18
Total number of alleles of both kinds = 180 + 18 = 198

Frequency of *Th* = $\dfrac{180}{198}$ = 0·9091 in the next generation

Frequency of *th* = $\dfrac{18}{198}$ = 0·0909 in the next generation

In example 5 we see that with the death of the homozygous recessives, the frequency of the *th* allele has fallen while the frequency of *Th* has risen, but the change is small. Figure 1 shows the decline in the frequency of the recessive allele from q = 0·1 when the homozygous recessives fail to reproduce. It is apparent from the graph that the lower the frequency becomes, the slower its decline, because the homozygous recessives will be very rare. Nearly all of the recessive alleles are carried by heterozygotes (see also example 4). This makes it clear that it would take scores

Figure 1 *Graph to show changes in the frequency of an allele which is lethal when homozygous*

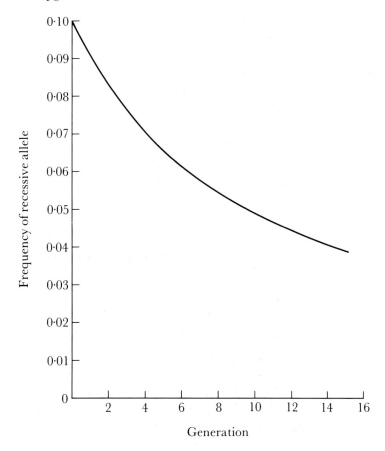

of generations to eliminate a recessive allele in a human population even if all homozygous individuals were to refrain from reproducing.

The equation and the equilibrium described in this chapter are both corollaries of the **Hardy–Weinberg Law** which states that in the absence of genetic drift, mutation, migration and selection, allele frequencies remain constant from generation to generation. It also states that if matings are at random, the genotype frequencies can be predicted by a simple formula (the Hardy–Weinberg equation). These genotype frequencies should be observed after a single generation of random mating (the population should reach Hardy–Weinberg equilibrium).

6.5 *Selection against deleterious recessive alleles*

Mutant alleles are normally recessive and when they first arise are present in the heterozygous state. Any offspring inheriting the allele will also be heterozygous and a recessive allele will increase in frequency before it appears in the homozygous state. As we saw in example 4, 1·4% of the British population is heterozygous for an allele which is homozygous in only one in 20 000 people. It has been estimated that almost everyone carries at least one deleterious (harmful) recessive allele in the heterozygous condition. Fortunately we have a low probability of marrying a person heterozygous for the same allele and thereby run the risk of producing homozygous children. However, if two people are related by descent, they may have inherited the same deleterious gene from a common ancestor. First cousins have one-eighth of their genes in common, genes which they have both inherited from their shared grandparents. The probability that a child of first cousins will be homozygous for an allele which is present in one of the grandparents is $\frac{1}{16}$. The term **inbreeding** is used to describe mating between individuals who are related by descent. The closest inbreeding possible is self fertilization which occurs in many species of plants.

In populations which normally inbreed, a recessive deleterious allele will appear in the homozygous state relatively soon after it has arisen by mutation. Natural selection will keep such genes at a very low frequency. A certain level of inbreeding is almost unavoidable in human populations living in isolated regions but as long as deleterious alleles are kept at a low frequency, the consequences of inbreeding in terms of hereditary abnormalities are minor. Where organisms are normally outbreeding, a deleterious allele can spread through a population in the heterozygous state. If such organisms then mate with close relatives, their progeny are more likely to be affected by inherited defects than are the progeny of individuals belonging to a population where inbreeding is the rule.

6.6 *Effects of human activity on allele frequencies in natural populations*

When environmental conditions change, so too may the selective pressures on a population. Human activity has been responsible for many environmental changes and their effects on allele frequencies have been well documented for several natural populations. Pollution by industry, contamination of soils by mining and the presence of pesticides are all examples of man-made change. While some populations have been exterminated by such activities, others have evolved in response to the new selection pressures. Evolution here means that an allele which was formerly rare has become more common. The allele may have been rare because it was not particularly advantageous to the organism which carried it or may even have been positively disadvantageous. But if environmental circumstances change, that allele may become beneficial and increase in frequency.

One of the first such evolutionary changes to be studied was the colouration of some species of moths which inhabit industrial regions polluted by smoke. About 80 species are known to have evolved a darker colour. In some cases, the darker colouring is under polygenic control but in others it is a single gene which is responsible for excess melanin (black pigment) production. Dark individuals, called **melanics**, occasionally arise in all kinds of animal species, e.g. the black panther which is a melanic form of the leopard. Melanic rabbits occur on the island of Skokholm off the coast of Wales but, like many melanics, they are at a disadvantage when compared with the wild type. The melanic rabbits are less well camouflaged than the agouti form and are more easily seen by predatory gulls.

In the Peppered Moth *Biston betularia* (Figure 2), melanism is caused by a dominant allele at a single locus. The moth rests by day flattened against exposed surfaces such as tree trunks or rocks where the pale, speckled form is camouflaged against the greyish lichens which are also found in such habitats. The pale moths show **cryptic colouration** in

Figure 2 *Typical and melanic forms of* Biston betularia

(a) Typical form

(b) Melanic form

these surroundings. A melanic moth contrasts with the background and so more easily falls prey to birds which hunt by sight such as spotted flycatchers, redstarts and robins. Melanics would be eliminated because the allele is dominant, so every individual which carries it will not be cryptically coloured.

Lichens are very susceptible to air pollution and few species grow near industrial areas, thus leaving dark tree bark uncovered. Soot from smoke settles on exposed surfaces and, during the nineteenth century, the habitat of the Peppered Moth became very grimy. The moth did not change its resting habits and it was the pale form which was no longer cryptically coloured. Environmental change caused the melanic to be at a selective advantage because it was now this form which was overlooked by predators. There was a reversal of the former situation with the melanics being more likely to survive and reproduce, so increasing the frequency of the allele for melanism in each successive generation. Records show that the frequency of melanic *Biston betularia* in Manchester increased to about 98% in 50 generations from 1848 when the first black specimen was captured. The percentage of melanics in various parts of Britain in the 1960s is shown in Figure 3 where it can be seen that the highest percentages are found in or near industrial centres. A similar distribution map for the 1970s indicates that the frequency of melanic forms has decreased slightly in most areas.

Figure 3 *The percentage of melanic forms of* Biston betularia *in populations in various regions of Britain in the 1960s*

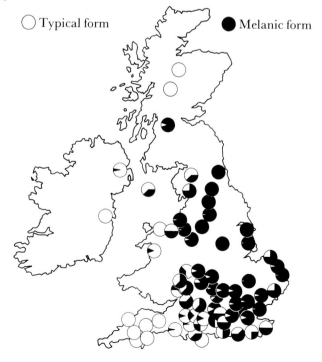

Where industry has been responsible for the rise in the frequency of melanic forms, the phenomenon is known as **industrial melanism**. Since the introduction of smokeless zones in the 1950s, the proportion of melanic *Biston betularia* is slowly declining. A few species of lichens are slowly recolonizing formerly polluted areas, surfaces are being cleaned and pale tree trunks are not being blackened by soot and so camouflaging backgrounds are again available to the pale form meaning that selection against them is not now so intense.

It must be appreciated that the allele for melanism in *Biston betularia* did not arise *because* of environmental pollution. The mutant allele arose spontaneously but because it was advantageous, natural selection caused it to increase in frequency. Similar examples of evolution include tolerance in grasses to the presence of heavy metal ions around mine workings, the resistance of rats to the poison warfarin and the resistance of mosquitoes to DDT. In some cases a gene with a major effect has been selected for and in other cases selection has been for a number of genes, each one contributing a little to the resistance. Even in *Biston betularia* where a dominant allele determines melanism, there has been selection for a number of modifier genes at different loci which intensify the dark colouring.

6.6.1 The Scalloped Hazel Moth exhibits industrial melanism. The dark colouring of the melanic form is inherited as a simple Mendelian dominant to the pale form.

(a) In a population where the two alleles M and m are in equal frequency, what will be the ratio of melanic:pale phenotypes at equilibrium?

(b) If 1000 moths in Hardy–Weinberg equilibrium are put into a heavily polluted environment where all the pale ones are eaten by predators but all the melanics survive, what will be the frequency of M and m in the survivors?

(c) If 1000 moths in Hardy–Weinberg equilibrium are put into a clean environment where all the melanics are taken by predators but all the pale ones survive, what will be the frequency of M and m in the survivors?

(d) Which allele is being selected against in (i) the polluted environment; (ii) the clean environment?

(e) Selection is not always so extreme as to cause the death of all individuals with a particular phenotype. Even so, would a deleterious gene be eliminated more rapidly if it is dominant or if it is recessive?

6.7 *Polymorphism and evolution*

Where two or more forms of the same species co-exist, the population is said to be **polymorphic** ('poly' means many and 'morph' means form). Most populations of any species show some discontinuous phenotypic variation and so it is usual to describe the type of polymorphism. Thus we speak of blood group or eye colour polymorphism in human populations. The term need not be restricted to variation which has a genetic basis. Ants and termites, for instance, have morphologically different castes but these are due to the way that the larvae are raised and not to genetic differences. However, unless otherwise stated, polymorphism normally refers to genetic polymorphism which may broadly be defined as the existence of more than one allele at a gene locus. The alleles in question bring about well-defined discontinuous variation in the phenotype; after all, this is how their existence is established. However, the polymorphism may not be a conspicuous one. Enzyme polymorphism is often only revealed by the laboratory technique of electrophoresis which can separate out different proteins from a mixture. Such studies have revealed that, on average, one-third or more loci in a large population are polymorphic. At some of these loci, the allele frequencies may be in the process of changing, as has happened in the case of industrial melanism in *Biston betularia*. This kind of polymorphism is described as **transient** because it is assumed that, in time, one allele will completely replace any others and the polymorphism will cease to exist. In other cases, the polymorphism has existed for a very long time and allele frequencies remain more or less constant. An example of such **stable** or **balanced** polymorphism is the banding patterns of the shells of the land snail *Cepaea nemoralis*. Shells which are over 6000 years old have been collected from British Neolithic sites and show the same variation in phenotypes as modern populations.

Transient polymorphism is evidence of evolution since evolution involves a change in allele frequencies. It is important to realize that evolution occurs within a species, indeed within a population. Many biologists would argue that the evolution of a new species is brought about by the accumulation, over thousands of generations, of small genetic differences between two isolated populations exposed to different selection pressures. Genetic variation is a prerequisite for evolution and in this book we have seen how it arises, how it is transmitted and how it can be analysed at the level of the population, but we have only touched on the role of genetic variation and natural selection in evolution.

6.8 Summary

The Hardy–Weinberg Law states that, in the absence of genetic drift, mutation, migration and selection, allele frequencies in a large, randomly mating, sexually reproducing population will remain the same from generation to generation. The genotype frequencies can be predicted from allele frequencies by the use of a formula known as the Hardy–Weinberg equation. A population in which genotype frequencies agree with those predicted by the formula is said to be in Hardy–Weinberg equilibrium. If a population is not in equilibrium, it may be because

(a) it is small,
(b) it is not randomly mating,
(c) one allele mutates to another more often than in the reverse direction,
(d) there is immigration into or emigration out of the population,
(e) selection is operating.

Selection, whether artificial or natural, increases the frequency of one allele at the expense of another. This is an evolutionary change and natural selection might be expected to improve a population's adaptedness to its environment. A change in allele frequencies proceeds more rapidly if it is a dominant allele which confers the selective advantage.

Industry, mining and pest control have been responsible for changing habitats and therefore altering the selection pressures on populations living in them. Excellent examples of directional change in allele frequencies are afforded by industrial melanism in several species of moths. Many species are made extinct by changes in their environment because they do not possess potentially advantageous genetic variation. The environment does not induce the formation of appropriate new alleles; it only selects from already existing variation.

Studies have shown that large populations may be polymorphic at about one-third of their gene loci. Such a reserve of genetic variation may prove to be a valuable asset should a population experience a change in selection pressures.

Key words

	Section		Section
artificial selection	6.4	inbreeding	6.5
balanced polymorphism	6.7	industrial melanism	6.6
cryptic colouration	6.6	melanic	6.6
gene pool	6.1	natural selection	6.4
genetic drift	6.4	polymorphism	6.7
Hardy–Weinberg equation	6.1	stable polymorphism	6.7
Hardy–Weinberg equilibrium	6.3	transient	
Hardy–Weinberg Law	6.4	polymorphism	6.7

Answers

6.4.1   (a) The genotypic ratio in the offspring of a self fertilizing heterozygote
Aa is 1 *AA* : 2 *Aa* : 1 *aa*. Out of 40 progeny, 10 are *AA*, 20 are *Aa* and 10
are *aa*.

(b) Total number of alleles = 2 × 40 = 80
Number of *A* alleles = (2 × 10) + 20 = 40
Number of *a* alleles = (2 × 10) + 20 = 40
Frequency of *A* = frequency of *a* = 0·5.

(c) The 10 *AA* plants have 400 *AA* progeny. The 10 *aa* plants have 400
aa progeny. The 20 *Aa* plants have 800 progeny of which 0·25 are *AA*,
0·5 are *Aa* and 0·25 are *aa* (as calculated in part (a)). The progeny of
the heterozygotes are therefore 200 *AA*, 400 *Aa* and 200 *aa*. Total
number of homozygotes = 400 + 400 + 200 + 200 = 1200

(d) The 1600 progeny are 600 *AA*, 600 *aa* and 400 *Aa*.
There are 2 × 1600 = 3200 alleles.
Number of *A* alleles = (2 × 600) + 400 = 1600
Number of *a* alleles = (2 × 600) + 400 = 1600
Frequency of *A* = frequency of *a* = 0·5

(e) The F_2 generation is not in Hardy–Weinberg equilibrium although
the allele frequencies have not changed. Self fertilization, a form of
inbreeding, has led to an excess of homozygotes.

6.6.1   (a) Frequency of *M* = p = 0·5. Frequency of *m* = q = 0·5.
At equilibrium the genotype frequencies will be 0·25 *MM*, 0·5 *Mm*
and 0·25 *mm*, according to the Hardy–Weinberg equation. Therefore
the phenotypic ratio is 0·75 melanic : 0·25 pale.

(b) 250 *mm* moths will be destroyed leaving 250 *MM* and 500 *Mm*.
Number of alleles left = (2 × 750) = 1500
Number of *M* alleles = (2 × 250) + 500 = 1000
Number of *m* alleles = 500
Frequency of *M* = $\frac{1000}{1500}$ = 0·667
Frequency of *m* = $\frac{500}{1500}$ = 0·333

(c) Out of 1000 moths, 250 *mm* survive. There are no melanics so the
frequency of *m* = 1·0.

(d) (i) *m*; (ii) *M*.

(e) Dominant.

PROBLEMS

66 Phenylketonuria is a hereditary disease of humans which, if untreated, may result in severe mental retardation. Phenylketonurics are homozygous recessive and occur at a frequency of one in 10 000 births.

(a) In a population of 1000, how many people would be expected to be heterozygous?

(b) A normal couple have already had one phenylketonuric child. What is the probability that their second child will be heterozygous for the condition?

67 The Duffy blood group system is controlled by a pair of alleles Fy^a and Fy^b. Duffy positive people have the genotype Fy^a/Fy^a or Fy^a/Fy^b while those with the genotype Fy^b/Fy^b are Duffy negative. In Britain, the Fy^b allele occurs in the frequency 0·6. If the population is in Hardy–Weinberg equilibrium for the Duffy alleles, what are the expected proportions of the three genotypes?

68 The ability to taste phenylthiocarbamide (PTC) is dominant to inability to taste. 252 Welsh people were tested and the following results were found.

	Tasters	Non-tasters	Total
Male	98	31	129
Female	104	19	123
Total	202	50	252

(a) Calculate the frequency of the recessive allele amongst
(i) males, (ii) females.

(b) The gene is not sex linked. What is the most probable explanation of the sex difference in this small sample?

69   Sickle cell anaemia is a serious hereditary disease and sufferers are homozygous for an allele, Hb^S, which codes for abnormal haemoglobin. Normal haemoglobin is coded for by the allele Hb^A. The heterozygotes $Hb^A Hb^S$ are healthy but can be recognized by the shape of their red blood cells. They have what is known as sickle cell trait.

(a) In an area of Central Africa, 2·5% of newborn babies have sickle cell anaemia. What is the frequency of the Hb^S allele in this population?

(b) How many of 500 babies are expected to be heterozygous?

70   In the Andalusian fowl, feather colour is determined by a pair of codominant alleles. Heterozygotes are 'blue' and homozygotes are either black or white. A smallholder bought a blue cock and some blue hens.

(a) 64 chicks were raised from these birds. How many of them are expected to be white?

(b) The smallholder ate all the original birds and sold all their white progeny. The remaining black and blue progeny were allowed to interbreed at random. What proportion of the next generation will be white?

71   Knowledge of the inheritance of the rhesus blood group system has saved many lives. Blood containing the rhesus antigen is rhesus positive (Rh^+) and is due to the presence of a dominant allele D. Rhesus negative people (Rh^-) have the genotype dd. If a Rh^- woman is pregnant with a Rh^+ child, the child could die before or soon after birth due to an immunological reaction of the mother against the foetus. Children at risk can be identified by finding out the blood groups of the parents and appropriate action can be taken to save the child's life.

(a) If the mother is Rh^-, what father's genotypes will put her child at risk through rhesus incompatibility?

(b) The frequency of the d allele in Europe is 0·4. What is the probability that a woman who knows she is Rh^- will marry a man who may put her child at risk?

72   In cats, the sex linked allele for ginger (orange) colouring is epistatic to the effects of all other genes for colour so that homozygous females $(X^G X^G)$ and hemizygous males $(X^G Y)$ are ginger. Heterozygous females have patches of ginger fur amongst patches of black or tabby fur, whichever is determined by genes on the autosomes. These females are called tortoiseshell. The colour of $X^g X^g$ and $X^g Y$ cats is determined by autosomal genes. Metcalfe and Turner recorded the phenotypes of all the cats taken in by the RSPCA in York over a period of twelve months. Out of 352 females, 15 were ginger $(X^G X^G)$, 91 were tortoiseshell $(X^G X^g)$ and 246 were other colours $(X^g X^g)$. 334 males were also recorded.

(a) Calculate allele frequencies using the data for females only.

(b) Allele frequencies are the same in both sexes but males are hemizygous at this gene locus. How many of the male cats are ginger?

73   Malaria is caused by a protozoan blood parasite *Plasmodium* and in West Africa is an important cause of death. Where malaria is prevalent, the sickle cell allele Hb^S is maintained at a relatively high frequency because sickle cell heterozygotes $Hb^A Hb^S$ are resistant to malaria and are more likely to reproduce than are normal homozygotes. In one population Hb^S occurs in the frequency of 0·1.

(a) Out of 1000 newborn babies in this population, how many would there be of each of the three genotypes?

(b) In this population of 1000, all the sickle cell homozygotes and 20% of the normal homozygotes die before reproducing. What is the frequency of the Hb^S allele in the remaining population?

74   The rat poison 'warfarin' was introduced into Britain in 1953. Genetically determined resistance was discovered in a population of rats near Welshpool in 1960. Resistance to warfarin is conferred by a dominant allele *R*. In 1961, 51% of rats in one area were found to be resistant to the poison.

(a) What is the frequency of the *R* allele in this population?

(b) Calculate the expected number of *RR*, *Rr* and *rr* genotypes in a population of 100 animals.

(c) If all the non-resistant rats in this population are killed by warfarin before reproducing, what will be the frequency of non-resistant rats born in the next generation?

75   There are three genetically distinct colour phases in the Arctic Skua. The pale and the dark form are both homozygous and the intermediate form is heterozygous. An island population of these birds was found to contain 158 pale, 280 intermediate and 212 dark.

(a) What are the expected numbers of each phenotype if the population is in Hardy–Weinberg equilibrium?

(b) Using the chi-square method, determine whether the difference between observed and expected numbers is statistically significant. (When expected numbers are calculated by using the Hardy–Weinberg equation, χ^2 has only one degree of freedom.)

(c) Assuming that there is no selection against any of the colour forms, how can you account for the difference between the observed and expected numbers?

Tests

TEST A (Chapters 1 and 2)

A1 Two tall pea plants were labelled A and B. The stamens were removed from all the flowers on both plants and the stigmas were dusted with pollen taken from a short plant. Plant A produced 72 seeds and plant B produced 66 seeds. All the seeds germinated and grew to maturity. The 66 seeds from plant B all grew into tall plants. Some of the seeds from plant A grew into tall and some into short plants.
   (a) Using suitable symbols, give the genotypes of the short plants and tall plants A and B.
   (b) How many of plant A's progeny would you expect to be short?

A2 Some people secrete in their saliva antigens corresponding to their blood group while others do not. One pair of alleles controls the difference. On the basis of the pedigree in Figure 1, state whether the ability to secrete is dominant or recessive and give a reason for your answer.

Figure 1

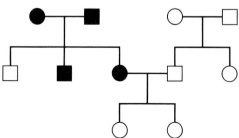

Key   Circles – females   Filled symbols – secretors
           Squares – males   Open symbols – non-secretors

A3 A variety of *Pelargonium* called Golden Crest has pale gold leaves. When plants of this variety are crossed together, the resulting seeds germinate as green, golden and white seedlings in the ratio 1 green : 2 golden : 1 white. The white seedlings are completely lacking in chlorophyll.
   (a) If golden plants are crossed to green plants, what phenotypes would appear in the progeny and in what proportions would they be expected?
   (b) A breeder wants to make a cross which would give all Golden Crest progeny. Is this possible? Explain your answer.

A4 In the pedigree in Figure 2, P is blood group O, R is group B and S is group AB. What is the probability that T is a girl with blood group B?

Figure 2

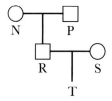

TEST B (Chapters 1–3)

B1 Maize plants homozygous for the recessive allele *wx* store amylopectin in their tissues while *Wx/wx* and *Wx/Wx* store normal starch. Amylopectin stains brown with iodine and normal starch stains blue-black. Pollen grains also contain either amylopectin or normal starch according to their own genotype. In an experiment, pollen was taken from a single anther of a heterozygous maize plant, placed on a microscope slide, stained with iodine and observed under the microscope. What would the observer see?
   A. All pollen grains the same colour.
   B. 75% pollen grains blue-black and 25% brown.
   C. 50% pollen grains blue-black and 50% brown.

B2 Guinea pigs are normally smooth haired. A fancier had bred them for many generations and always got smooth haired ones. He borrowed a rough haired animal and mated it to a smooth haired one of his own. The resulting litter consisted of three rough and one smooth haired.
(a) Which is the dominant allele?
(b) Using suitable symbols, show the genotypes of the parent animals and of their litter.

B3 In the domestic fowl, two gene loci affecting feather colour are 'L' and 'D'. White Leghorn are *LL DD* where the presence of a dominant *L* allele causes white feathers. White Dorking are *ll dd* where the homozygous recessive *dd* is responsible for white feathers. Coloured birds have the genotypes *ll DD* or *ll Dd*.
(a) When White Leghorn is crossed to White Dorking, what will be the genotype and phenotype of the F$_1$ progeny?
(b) The F$_1$ birds are backcrossed to the White Dorking breed.
   (i) What is the genotypic ratio in the backcross progeny?
   (ii) What is the ratio of white: coloured in the backcross progeny?

B4 A study of the inheritance of vegetative characters of pears revealed the following pairs of alleles.

Character	Traits
Young shoot colour	Red (R) and green (r)
Hairiness of young shoot	Hairy (H) and hairless (h)
Leaf margin	Toothed (S) and untoothed (s)
Leaf colour	Dark green (G) and pale green (g)

Different varieties of pears were found to have the following genotypes.

Variety	Genotype			
Comice	Rr	SS	hh	Gg
Williams	rr	Ss	hh	GG
Conference	rr	Ss	hh	Gg
Beurré Hardy	Rr	Ss	Hh	GG

Pears are self incompatible, i.e. self pollination does not result in fertilization.

(a) A child ate a Conference pear and planted one of the pips. The seedling had red, hairless shoots and toothed, pale green leaves. Which variety was the male parent of the seed?

(b) If Conference and Williams were crossed, what proportion of their progeny would have untoothed leaves?

(c) If Beurré Hardy and Comice were crossed, what proportion of their progeny would have red, hairy shoots?

(d) If Williams and Beurré Hardy were crossed, how many different combinations of traits could occur in their offspring?

TEST C (Chapters 1–3)

C1 Persian cats have long hair. Siamese cats have short hair which is pale except for dark points (nose, feet, ears and tail). A breeder with genetical knowledge realized that a new 'Persian-Siamese' breed could be produced which would be pure breeding for long hair with the Siamese colouring. She started her breeding programme by crossing a pure bred black Persian female with a pure bred Siamese male and obtained two F_1 kittens, one male and one female. They were both black and short haired. She crossed these F_1 animals and obtained only one F_2 kitten, a black, long haired female.

(a) What is the probability of obtaining a 'Persian-Siamese' kitten in the F_2 generation?

(b) The F_2 female was backcrossed to her grandfather. She proved to be heterozygous at the coat colour locus. What are the possible phenotypes in her litter?

(c) Using suitable symbols give the possible genotypes of the kittens in her progeny.

(d) How should the breeder proceed in order to get 'Persian-Siamese' kittens? Assume that there are sufficient animals of the appropriate kinds in the backcross progeny.

C2 In humans, wavy hair is dominant to straight and free ear lobe is dominant to fixed. A married couple are heterozygous for both characters. What is the probability that

(a) their first child will have fixed ear lobes;

(b) their first daughter will have free ear lobes and wavy hair;

(c) their next child will be a boy with straight hair and free ear lobes?

C3 Bay horses have a brownish coat with black mane, tail, muzzle and 'socks'. The phenotype is controlled by two gene loci and bay has the genotype *BB II*. Chestnut horses (genotype *bb ii*) are brown all over. When bay is crossed to chestnut the offspring are all bay. The genotypes and phenotypes obtained from crossing together double heterozygotes are shown in the table.

Bay	Chestnut	Black
BB II	*bb ii*	*BB ii*
Bb II	*bb Ii*	*Bb ii*
BB Ii	*bb II*	
Bb Ii		

(a) In what ratio should chestnut, black and bay horses occur in an F_2 generation?

(b) Describe how the two gene loci interact to produce the three coat colours.

C4 *Phlox drummondii* is an annual plant commonly grown in gardens. The usual variety has broad petals and there are two star shaped varieties called 'cuspidata' and 'fimbriata'. This flower shape character is controlled by a single gene locus. A second locus controls whether the petals lie flat or in the shape of a funnel. Two plants were crossed and their progeny appeared in the following numbers:

broad petals, flat	35
broad petals, funnel	10
'cuspidata', flat	30
'cuspidata', funnel	13
'fimbriata', flat	70
'fimbriata', funnel	22

(a) What were the phenotypes and genotypes of the parents of these progeny? Define your gene symbols.

(b) What are the genotypes of the six classes of progeny?

TEST D (*Chapters 1–5*)

D1 The recessive genes for haemophilia and red–green colour-blindness are both sex linked. A woman whose father was a haemophiliac but had normal colour vision has a son who is red–green colour-blind but has normal blood. Like his mother, the second son is neither a haemophiliac nor colour-blind. Explain how the two brothers have inherited their sex linked traits.

D2 The coat colour of the English setter is controlled by two gene loci, 'B' and 'E'. Presence of at least one dominant allele at each locus results in black fur. The double homozygous recessive has yellow fur. Animals with the genotypes *Bb ee* and *BB ee* are red while *bb Ee* and *bb EE* are liver brown.
   (a) A black bitch was mated to the same liver brown dog on several occasions and produced a total of 14 pups of which there were 2 yellow, 3 red, 4 liver and 5 black. What were the genotypes of the parents?
   (b) A breeder has a yellow bitch and wants to get litters of only black and red pups in approximately equal numbers. What should be the phenotype and genotype of the father?
   (c) A breeder has a champion liver coloured dog whose mother was yellow. The dog is mated to a red bitch who has the same mother. What are the possible colours of their offspring and in what proportions would they be expected?

D3 Manx cats have a deformed pelvis and are usually completely tailless. The condition is caused by a single dominant gene. The homozygous dominant dies *in utero* and is reabsorbed. What proportion of the litter produced by a pair of Manx cats are expected to be tailless?

D4 A *Drosophila* geneticist had three stocks of homozygous flies. Stock A had normal wings, stock B had very short wings and stock C had full length but narrow wings. The results of three sets of crosses are given below.

Cross 1: stock A × stock B	Cross 2: stock A × stock C
F_1 all normal	F_1 all normal
F_2 $\frac{3}{4}$ normal, $\frac{1}{4}$ very short wings	F_2 $\frac{3}{4}$ normal, $\frac{1}{4}$ full length, narrow wings

Cross 3: stock B × stock C

F_1 all half-length, narrow wings

F_2 $\frac{1}{2}$ half-length, narrow wings

$\frac{1}{4}$ very short wings

$\frac{1}{4}$ full length, narrow wings

(a) How many gene loci control the wing shape character?

(b) Using suitable symbols, suggest genotypes for the flies of stocks A, B and C.

(c) Explain the results of the third cross.

TEST E (Chapters 1–5)

E1 Cleidocranial dysostosis is a rare developmental disease which is due to a dominant autosomal gene. An affected person has skeletal abnormalities including lack of clavicles (collar bones). An affected man whose mother was normal has married a normal woman.

(a) What is the probability that their first child will be a normal girl?

(b) What is the probability that their first two children will both be affected?

E2 In 1921 Eyster reported the results of a series of crosses with maize which he carried out in order to discover the linkage relations of the genes then known in this species. One of his crosses involved the gene for starchy seeds (S) and its allele for sugary seeds (s) and also the gene for liguleless leaf (lg) and its allele for normal leaf (Lg). (The ligule on a grass leaf is a membranous outgrowth where the blade joins the part which sheaths the stem.) Eyster crossed doubly heterozygous plants grown from starchy seeds and whose leaves had ligules (genotype $S/s \ Lg/lg$) with double homozygous recessive plants. The resulting seeds were either starchy or sugary and grew into plants with or without ligules, in the following numbers.

Phenotype	Number
Starchy, normal leaves	683
Starchy, liguleless	652
Sugary, normal leaves	376
Sugary, liguleless	379

Explain these results, stating whether there is any evidence for linkage between the two loci.

E3 There is a sex linked gene in the mouse called *tabby* (Ta). When heterozygous, it causes striped (tabby) markings in the fur. When homozygous or hemizygous, it causes the fur to appear greasy but not striped. The normal coat is neither greasy nor striped.

(a) Show diagrammatically the expected offspring phenotypes and genotypes of a cross between a striped female and a greasy male.

(b) If you have only normal females and greasy males, show diagrammatically the breeding programme you could use to produce greasy females in as few generations as possible. (Mice can be bred to close relatives.)

E4 A laboratory has two stocks of the shrimp, *Gammarus*. Both stock 1 and stock 2 have red eyes and are pure breeding. When the two stocks were crossed together, all the F_1 progeny had black eyes which is the wild type colour. The F_1 shrimps were allowed to interbreed. The F_2 progeny consisted of 585 black eyed and 451 red eyed shrimps.
(a) Explain why all the F_1 progeny had black eyes.
(b) Define gene symbols and give all possible genotypes of the 451 red eyed F_2 animals.

TEST F (Chapters 1–6)

F1 The table below shows the number of M, MN and N blood groups in a sample of Sikhs.

Genotype	Phenotype	Number
$L^M L^M$	Group M	89
$L^M L^N$	Group MN	95
$L^N L^N$	Group N	29

(a) Calculate the frequency of the L^M and L^N alleles.
(b) Is this population in Hardy–Weinberg equilibrium?

F2 A white eyed female *Gammarus* (a shrimp) was mated to a red eyed male. The F_1 progeny consisted of 3 black eyed and 6 red eyed shrimps. The black eyed ones were two females and a male. The total number of F_2 young obtained from mating the black eyed male to the black eyed females was 120 of which 66 were black eyed, 23 red eyed and 31 white eyed. The eye colour is controlled by two gene loci, each with two alleles.
(a) What is the approximate ratio of phenotypes in the F_2 progeny?
(b) Explain how the two loci interact with each other to produce the three eye colours.
(c) Using suitable symbols, suggest genotypes for the original white eyed female and red eyed male.

F3 Mice with the genotype *a'/a We/we B/b* were crossed to *a/a we/we b/b*. The genotypes of the progeny and their numbers are given in the table below.

Genotype	Number	Genotype	Number
a/a We/we B/b	4	*a'/a We/we B/b*	41
a/a We/we b/b	8	*a'/a We/we b/b*	34
a/a we/we B/b	36	*a'/a we/we B/b*	9
a/a we/we b/b	42	*a'/a we/we b/b*	4

Which of the loci are linked? Show your reasoning.

F4 Collie dogs are normally tan, black and white. Another colour type is called blue merle, where the coat is blue grey and pale tan with irregular black patches. Blue merle animals have smoky grey eyes. The following table shows the phenotypes of the progeny from a number of crosses between blue merles.

Coat colour	Tan, black, white	Blue merle	White
Eye colour	Dark	Smoky grey	Pale
Number of progeny	20	39	20

(a) Suggest a simple hypothesis to account for the observed mode of inheritance of coat colour in collies.

(b) Give **two** reasons to account for the association of eye colour with coat colour.

TEST G (Chapters 1–6)

G1 A variety of peas called 'First of All' is susceptible to mildew, a disease caused by the fungus *Erysiphe*. First of All has white flowers. In a second, purple flowered variety, collected from a Peruvian village called Huancabamba, about 10% of the plants were immune to mildew. Some of the immune Huancabamba plants were crossed with susceptible First of All. The F_1 plants had purple flowers and were all susceptible. Two F_2 families were grown of which 178 plants were susceptible and 62 were immune. When immune plants were crossed together, all their progeny were immune.

(a) Is immunity to mildew a dominant or a recessive trait?

(b) How do the data demonstrate that a single gene locus controls immunity/susceptibility?

(c) The gene locus controlling immunity/susceptibility ('Er') was found to be linked to the locus controlling flower colour ('A'). Using the symbolism for linked genes, show the genotype of the F_1 hybrids. Bear in mind the origin of the allele for immunity.

G2 A population of the snail *Cepaea nemoralis*, collected in sand dunes in Northumberland, was found to consist of

      76 pink, banded
    245 pink, unbanded
    370 yellow, banded
    35 yellow, unbanded

Pink (C^P) is dominant to yellow (C^Y), and unbanded (B) is dominant to banded (b).

(a) Present the data above in the form of a table with two columns and two rows. Supply column and row totals and a grand total.

(b) Assume the population is in Hardy–Weinberg equilibrium.
  (i) Calculate the frequencies of C^P and C^Y.
  (ii) Calculate the frequencies of B and b.

G3 In the Suffolk breed of sheep, neither sex has horns. In the Dorset breed, both sexes are horned. The presence or absence of horns is determined by alleles at a single gene locus and both breeds are homozygous. Both reciprocal crosses between the two breeds give horned F_1 males and hornless F_1 females. The gene locus involved is *not* sex linked. In an F_2 generation, what would be the ratio of horned to hornless in (a) males, (b) females?

G4 A biology teacher has three pairs of gerbils. One pair is agouti ($AA\ CC$), the second pair is black ($aa\ CC$) and the third pair is albino ($AA\ cc$). She wants to get gerbils which will give offspring in the ratio
     9 agouti : 3 black : 4 albino
(a) What is the simplest breeding programme to produce the required animals?
(b) The teacher succeeded in getting animals of the required genotypes. When she crossed them, their first litter consisted of one black and two agouti. What is the probability that the black one was heterozygous for albinism?

TEST H (Chapters 1–6)

H1 In parts of Wales, the frequency of I^O, one of the alleles determining the ABO blood groups, is 70%. Use the Hardy–Weinberg formula to calculate the proportion of people in these areas who are not blood group O.

H2 Dalmatian dogs excrete a high level of uric acid while other breeds excrete only small amounts. The difference is controlled by two alleles at a single gene locus and low level of excretion is dominant to high. Dalmatians are also homozygous for an allele which causes spotted coat. When Dalmatians are crossed to collies, the F_1 animals show some spotting and all excrete low levels of uric acid. A breeding experiment was carried out to discover whether the locus for uric acid excretion is linked to the locus for spotting. The two breeds were crossed and the F_1 progeny were backcrossed to Dalmatians. The backcross progeny were as follows.

Phenotype	Number
Some spotting, low uric acid	2
Some spotting, high uric acid	5
Fully spotted, low uric acid	6
Fully spotted, high uric acid	2

From these results, is there any evidence for linkage? Explain your answer.

H3 Rex rabbits have short, soft, wavy hair and curly whiskers. The rex phenotype was discovered by Abbé Gillet in France in 1919 as a newly arisen mutant. In 1927, Madame Du Bary found that some of her rabbits were producing rex offspring. Both Abbé Gillet and Madame Du Bary discovered that their rex rabbits were homozygous for the trait but when the Gillet and Du Bary rabbits were crossed together, all the progeny had normal hair. How can you explain this?

H4 Figure 3 shows the inheritance of glucose-6-phosphate dehydrogenase (G6PD) deficiency in two unrelated families. In an Afghan population, 10% of males were found to be G6PD deficient. What would be the expected frequency of G6PD deficient females in this population?

Figure 3

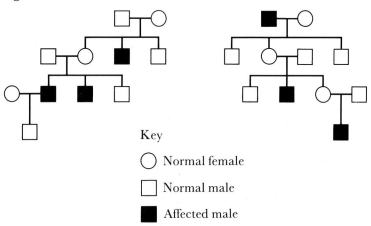

Key

◯ Normal female

☐ Normal male

■ Affected male

Answers to problems

1 Monohybrid inheritance (1)

1 (a) Starchy, as this is the dominant trait.
  (b) The cobs on the F_1 plants contain the seeds of the F_2 generation which should be in the ratio 3 starchy : 1 sugary.

2 The heterozygous F_1 plants have green pods so green is dominant to yellow. The 580 plants should occur in the ratio 3 green : 1 yellow. $\frac{3}{4} \times 580 = 435$. $\frac{1}{4} \times 580 = 145$. Therefore 435 should be green and 145 should be yellow.

3 The ratio in the F_2 generation is 3 erect : 1 hooded. Erect must be dominant. Therefore the F_1 plants had erect flowers.

4 882 were inflated, therefore 299 were constricted. $\frac{882}{299} = 2.95$. Therefore the ratio in the F_2 generation is 2·95 inflated : 1 constricted.

5 (a) The unbanded snails had banded progeny so the parents were not pure breeding. They were heterozygous, Uu.
  (b) Unbanded progeny are either Uu ($\frac{2}{3}$) or UU ($\frac{1}{3}$).

6 No. Although he carries the recessive allele for the disease, he has a normal, dominant allele at the same locus, so he will be normal.

7 (a) Heterozygote has short hair. Homozygous recessive is Angora.
  (b) Short hair, Ss; Angora ss.
  (c) Half.

8 The agouti parents are not pure breeding, so they are heterozygous. Agouti is dominant (the phenotype of the parents) so their progeny should appear in the ratio 3 agouti : 1 black.

9 The two parental plants are heterozygous for small size because $\frac{1}{4}$ of their progeny are small. Of the normal progeny, $\frac{2}{3}$ will be heterozygous and therefore would be expected to have some small sized progeny after self fertilization.

10 (a) Herbert's offspring would have a white face. Larry's would not.
  (b) Half the calves would have a white face and the other half would not.

11 1 normal : 1 waltzer.

12 The woman is Ww and her husband is ww. Their children can be either Ww or ww. There is a 1 in 2 chance that her first child will have white forelock (Ww).

2 *Monohybrid inheritance (2)*

13   Roan is the heterozygous condition and is a result of codominance between the two alleles.
(a) $\frac{1}{4}$ white, $\frac{1}{2}$ roan, $\frac{1}{4}$ red;   (b) $\frac{1}{2}$ roan, $\frac{1}{2}$ white;   (c) $\frac{1}{2}$ roan, $\frac{1}{2}$ red.

14   The parents had children who could not roll their tongues so inability to roll one's tongue is recessive and the parents were heterozygous (Rr). The 'roller' children are RR or Rr and the 'non-roller' children are rr. 3 rollers:1 non-roller is the theoretical expectation but in a small family a perfect ratio is not always obtained.

15   (a) Recessive because normal parents had thalassaemic children.
(b) *Th* represents the normal allele and *th* represents the allele for thalassaemia (Table 1).

Table 1

		Gametes from mother	
		Th	*th*
Gametes	*Th*	*Th/Th*	*Th/th*
from father	*th*	*Th/th*	*th/th*

We know Carmen is not *th/th*. She has a $\frac{2}{3}$ chance of being heterozygous.
(c) The probability that Mario is heterozygous is also $\frac{2}{3}$. Only if they are both heterozygous can they have a thalassaemic child..
$$P(\text{both heterozygous}) = \tfrac{2}{3} \times \tfrac{2}{3} = \tfrac{4}{9}$$
The probability that two heterozygotes will have a thalassaemic child is $\frac{1}{4}$. Therefore the probability that Carmen and Mario will have a thalassaemic child is
$$\tfrac{4}{9} \times \tfrac{1}{4} = \tfrac{4}{36} = \tfrac{1}{9}$$

16   Cobalt is the heterozygous condition (c^1c^2). By breeding Cobalts together, he would get $\frac{1}{4}$ Mauve (c^1c^1), $\frac{1}{2}$ Cobalt (c^1c^2) and $\frac{1}{4}$ Skyblue (c^2c^2).

17   (a) $\frac{1063}{535} = 1 \cdot 99$. The ratio is approximately 2 yellow:1 non-yellow.
(b) This ratio suggests that yellow is dominant to non-yellow. Carry out a testcross to the homozygous recessive (non-yellow). A heterozygous mouse should have some non-yellow progeny but a homozygous yellow mouse would have only yellow progeny.
(c) Yellow.
(d) Non-yellow.

18 Spotted no. 1 is heterozygous (*Ss*) because it has unspotted progeny when crossed to spotted no. 3, which must also be *Ss*. Spotted no. 2 is *SS* because it has no unspotted progeny when crossed to *Ss*. All the unspotted ones are *ss*.

19 (a) If Tonkinese can produce both Burmese and Siamese, Tonkinese is heterozygous (t^1t^2). Siamese is t^1t^1 and Burmese is t^2t^2.

    (b) (i) Siamese × Siamese;   (ii) Burmese × Burmese;   (iii) Siamese × Burmese.

20 (a) Recessive because normal × ichthyotic gives all normal progeny.

    (b) 5·3:1 and 3:1.

    (c) We would expect ratios of 3:1 in the second cross and 1:1 in the third cross. Ichthyotic is not occurring as frequently as expected. It is not lethal when homozygous but it reduces viability.

21 The parents must be heterozygous for I^O to have a group O son. The mother is group A and so is genotype I^AI^O. The daughter with group B must have inherited I^B from her father who must be genotype I^BI^O.

22 (a) All brown; (b) $\frac{1}{2}$ brown, $\frac{1}{2}$ pink; (c) $\frac{3}{4}$ brown, $\frac{1}{4}$ pink; (d) $\frac{1}{2}$ pink, $\frac{1}{2}$ yellow; (e) $\frac{1}{2}$ brown, $\frac{1}{4}$ pink, $\frac{1}{4}$ yellow.

23 Clearwing × full colour gives full colour, clearwing and dilute progeny. Dilute is recessive to all the others so both the clearwing and full colour parents must have carried c^d. Parents were therefore c^w/c^d and C/c^d.

    (a) $\frac{1}{4}$

    (b) Probability of one bird being full colour = $\frac{1}{2}$

        P(both full colour) = $\frac{1}{2} \times \frac{1}{2} = \frac{1}{4}$

24 The type of fruit depends on the genotype of the parent tree.

    (a) Peach could be dominant (*P*) and the nectarine recessive (*p*). A peach tree could be heterozygous (*Pp*) and its flowers could have been pollinated by *p* bearing pollen. The seed inside the fruit could have the genotype *pp* and would grow into a nectarine bearing tree. The flowers of nectarine trees (*pp*) could be pollinated with *P* bearing pollen and the seeds (*Pp*) would grow into peach bearing trees. A similar argument holds if nectarine is dominant. (Nectarine is in fact recessive.)

    (b) If both parents are homozygous, crossing peach with nectarine would give all peach or all nectarine, whichever is dominant.

        If one of the trees is homozygous recessive and the other is heterozygous, on crossing, half the progeny would be peach and half would be nectarine. It would not be possible to say which was the homozygous parent. Therefore, at the same time as crossing two different plants, some of the flowers on each plant should be selfed. If one of the trees should prove to be heterozygous it can be recognised because its progeny should include some that are unlike the parent plant while the homozygous recessive would breed true.

25 The baby's genotype is $I^O I^O$. Miss X is group A so is genotype $I^A I^O$. The baby cannot belong to Y who is genotype $I^A I^B$, but Z must be $I^B I^O$.

3 Dihybrid inheritance

26 (a) $AA\,bb \times aa\,BB$; (b) $aa\,Bb \times Aa\,bb$; (c) $Aa\,Bb \times Aa\,Bb$.

27 (a) Tall with grey seeds. (b) Genotype of F_1 plants is $Tt\,Gg$. When these are selfed, the F_2 progeny will be 9 tall, grey : 3 tall, white : 3 short, grey : 1 short, white.

28 (a) Parents are $Cc\,Hh$.
   $P(Cc) = \frac{1}{2}$ and P $(Hh) = \frac{1}{2}$. Therefore P $(Cc\,Hh) = \frac{1}{2} \times \frac{1}{2} = \frac{1}{4}$
   (b) P(normal leaf) $= \frac{3}{4}$ and P(hairless) $= \frac{1}{4}$
   Therefore P(normal leaf, hairless) $= \frac{3}{4} \times \frac{1}{4} = \frac{3}{16}$

29 (a) $P(CC) = \frac{1}{4}$ and P(hh) $= \frac{1}{2}$
   Therefore $P(CC\,hh) = \frac{1}{4} \times \frac{1}{2} = \frac{1}{8}$
   (b) P(potato leaf) $= \frac{1}{4}$ and P(hairless) $= \frac{1}{2}$
   Therefore P(potato leaf, hairless) $= \frac{1}{4} \times \frac{1}{2} = \frac{1}{8}$

30 The $\frac{3}{16}$ white, single combed consist of $\frac{2}{16}$ $Ww\,pp$ and $\frac{1}{16}$ $WW\,pp$. Only WW pp will have only white offspring. The probability that a white, single combed cock is $WW\,pp$ is $\frac{1}{3}$.

31 Let the locus for general colour be 'G' with the alleles G and g, and let the locus for intensity of colour be 'I' with the alleles i^1 and i^2.
   (a) $GG\,i^1i^1 \times gg\,i^1i^2$ gives 1 light green : 1 dark green.
   (b) $Gg\,i^2i^2 \times Gg\,i^2i^2$ gives 3 olive : 1 mauve.
   (c) $Gg\,i^1i^2 \times gg\,i^1i^2$ gives 1 light green : 2 dark green : 1 olive : 2 sky blue : 2 cobalt : 1 mauve.

32 The parents have the genotype $b^1b^2\,Ss$. The progeny will appear in the ratio 3 black, normal : 1 black, silky : 6 blue, normal : 2 blue, silky : 3 white, normal : 1 white, silky.

33 (a) $\frac{1}{9}\,(YY\,TT)$; (b) $\frac{2}{9}\,(YY\,Tt)$; (c) $\frac{4}{9}\,(Yy\,Tt)$; (d) $\frac{2}{9}\,(Yy\,TT)$.

34 Let Y represent the allele for yellow, y for green, S for smooth and s for wrinkled. The parents are $Yy\,Ss \times yy\,ss$ or $Yy\,ss \times yy\,Ss$.

35 Let the allele for phenylketonuria be p and the normal allele be P. The parents are genotypes $Pp\,I^O I^O$ and $Pp\,I^A I^B$.

   P(group A) $= \frac{1}{2}$
   P(phenylketonuria) $= \frac{1}{4}$
   Probability that child will have blood group A and
   phenylketonuria $= \frac{1}{2} \times \frac{1}{4} = \frac{1}{8}$

36 (a) White × dark red gives 1 wild type : 1 scarlet : 1 brown : 1 white.
   (b) Dark red × dark red gives 9 dark red : 3 scarlet : 3 brown : 1 white.
   (c) Scarlet × brown gives 1 dark red : 1 brown.

37 All dihybrid crosses can be treated as two monohybrid crosses. Look first at eye colour. $27 + 18 = 45$ are wild type and $5 + 10 = 15$ are scarlet. This is a ratio of $3:1$. Therefore the parents must both have been heterozygous for eye colour (St/st).

   $27 + 5 = 32$ have wild type legs and $18 + 10 = 28$ have gouty legs. This is a ratio of approximately $1:1$ so the parent with wild type legs must have been heterozygous.

   The parental genotypes were $St/st\ gy/gy$ (wild type eye colour, gouty legs) and $St/st\ Gy/gy$ (wild type eye colour, wild type legs).

38 Genotype of parents is $Aa\ Ee$ (phenotype – red). Black is obtained when the genotype is $aa\ EE$ or $aa\ Ee$. The proportion of offspring from this cross which are $aa\ EE$ or $aa\ Ee$ can be calculated using a Punnett square or the probability method (shown here).
   $P(aa) = \frac{1}{4}, \quad P(EE) = \frac{1}{4}, \quad P(Ee) = \frac{1}{2}$
   $P(aa\ EE) = \frac{1}{4} \times \frac{1}{4} = \frac{1}{16}$
   $P(aa\ Ee) = \frac{1}{4} \times \frac{1}{2} = \frac{1}{8}$
   $P(aa\ EE\ \text{or}\ aa\ Ee) = \frac{1}{16} + \frac{1}{8} = \frac{3}{16}$

39 Show the results of the $Ac/ac\ Li/li \times Ac/ac\ Li/li$ cross in a Punnett square (Table 2).

Table 2

		Gametes from male			
		Ac		*ac*	
		Li	*li*	*Li*	*li*
Ac	*Li*	*Ac/Ac Li/Li*	*Ac/Ac Li/li*	*Ac/ac Li/Li*	*Ac/ac Li/li*
	li	*Ac/Ac Li/li*	*Ac/Ac li/li*	*Ac/ac Li/li*	*Ac/ac li/li*
ac	*Li*	*Ac/ac Li/Li*	*Ac/ac Li/li*	*ac/ac Li/Li*	*ac/ac Li/li*
	li	*Ac/ac Li/li*	*Ac/ac li/li*	*ac/ac Li/li*	*ac/ac li/li*

(Gametes from female)

   (a) Cyanogenic plants must have *Ac* and *Li*. $\frac{9}{16} \times 1600 = 900$ have both of these. 700 have only one or neither.
   (b) $\frac{3}{16} \times 1600 = 300$ of the acyanogenic plants which are *ac/ac Li/Li* or *ac/ac Li/li* would produce HCN on addition of glucosides.
   (c) $\frac{3}{16} \times 1600 = 300$ of the acyanogenic plants which are *Ac/Ac li/li* or *Ac/ac li/li* would produce HCN on addition of the enzyme.
   (d) $\frac{1}{16} \times 1600 = 100$ have neither enzyme nor glucosides (*ac/ac li/li*).

40 (a) Show all the possible genotypes in a Punnett square. The $\frac{12}{16}$ with W are wire haired. Of the non-wire haired animals, both $ww\,KK$ and $ww\,kk$ are pure breeding and both constitute $\frac{1}{16}$ of the offspring so either could be the long haired ones. However, the $\frac{3}{16}$ short haired ones are most likely to be those with a K.

  (i) The long haired pups are $ww\,kk$.

  (ii) The short haired pups are $ww\,KK$ and $ww\,Kk$.

(b) The possible genotypes for wire haired are $WW\,KK$, $WW\,Kk$, $WW\,kk$, $Ww\,KK$, $Ww\,Kk$ and $Ww\,kk$. When crossed with a long haired bitch, Frank has some long haired offspring so he must be heterozygous at the 'W' locus. If Frank were $Ww\,KK$ or $Ww\,kk$ he would have only two types of offspring when paired with long haired bitches. By similar reasoning, long haired cannot be $ww\,KK$ (see (a) (i)). Frank must be $Ww\,Kk$.

$Ww\,Kk \times ww\,kk$ gives $1\ \underbrace{Ww\,Kk : 1\ Ww\,kk}_{\text{2 wire haired}} : \underset{\text{1 short}}{1\ ww\,Kk} : \underset{\text{1 long}}{1\ ww\,kk}$

4 Sex determination and sex linkage

41 See Table 3.

Table 3

	X^cX^c yellow female	$\times$	X^CY wild type male	
			Gametes from male	
			$\frac{1}{2}X^C$	$\frac{1}{2}Y$
Gametes from female	all X^c		$\frac{1}{2}X^CX^c$ $\frac{1}{2}$ wild type F_1 females	$\frac{1}{2}X^cY$ $\frac{1}{2}$ yellow F_1 males

	X^CX^c F_1 wild type female	$\times$	X^cY F_1 yellow male	
			Gametes from F_1 male	
			$\frac{1}{2}X^c$	$\frac{1}{2}Y$
Gametes from F_1 female	$\frac{1}{2}X^C$ $\frac{1}{2}X^c$		$\frac{1}{4}X^CX^c$ $\frac{1}{4}X^cX^c$	$\frac{1}{4}X^CY$ $\frac{1}{4}X^cY$

F_2 female progeny are in the ratio 1 yellow (X^cX^c) : 1 wild type (X^CX^c).

F_2 male progeny are in the ratio 1 yellow (X^cY) : 1 wild type (X^CY).

42   Queen Victoria, Alexandra, Victoria Eugenie, Alice of Hesse, Alice of Athlone, Irene and Beatrice.

43   Let h be the allele for haemophilia and let H be the wild type allele. Both parents must transmit h to a haemophiliac daughter. The father is X^hY and the mother is most likely X^HX^h as X^hX^h females are very rare and do not normally live to adulthood.

44   The boy inherited his X-chromosome from his mother, so it must be his mother's father who is colour-blind.

45   (a) The brother is X^dY and has inherited X^d from his mother. The probability that his sister has inherited the same chromosome is $\frac{1}{2}$.
   (b) She has transmitted X^d to her son so she must be heterozygous. The probability that the second son will be affected is $\frac{1}{2}$.

46   (a) (i) X^GX^G (ginger female) $\times$ X^gY (black male);   (ii) X^gX^g (black female) $\times$ X^GY (ginger male).
   (b) (i) ginger;   (ii) black.
   (c) The infertile female is X^g0. The sperm which fused with the ovum to form the zygote did not carry a sex chromosome.

47   The male and female phenotypic ratios are different in the progeny suggesting that the gene is sex linked. Males constitute only one-third instead of one-half of the progeny and they are all wild type. This suggests that *notched* is lethal in males. Notched females must be heterozygous because their female progeny are either wild type or notched. The cross made was X^NX^n (notched female) $\times$ X^nY (wild type male) (Table 4).

Table 4

		Gametes from male	
		$\frac{1}{2}X^n$	$\frac{1}{2}Y$
Gametes from female	$\frac{1}{2}X^N$	$\frac{1}{4}X^NX^n$	$\frac{1}{4}X^NY$
	$\frac{1}{2}X^n$	$\frac{1}{4}X^nX^n$	$\frac{1}{4}X^nY$

F_1 progeny are $\frac{1}{4}X^NX^n$ notched females $\Big\}\frac{2}{3}$ females
$\qquad\qquad\quad \frac{1}{4}X^nX^n$ wild type females
$\qquad\qquad\quad \frac{1}{4}X^nY$ wild type males $-\frac{1}{3}$ males
$\qquad\qquad\quad \frac{1}{4}X^NY$ die

48   Cross barred females (X^BY) to unbarred males (X^bX^b). All the male chicks will have a white spot (X^BX^b) and the female chicks will not (X^bY).

49

$$X^cY \qquad\qquad X^CX^C$$

cinnamon female × black male

$$X^CY \qquad\qquad X^CX^c \qquad\qquad X^cY$$

black females and black males × cinnamon female

$$X^CX^c \qquad X^CY \qquad X^cX^c \qquad X^cY$$

black males black females cinnamon males × cinnamon females

↓

all cinnamon offspring

50 The allele for black is on the Y-chromosome.

Black female (XY^B) × wild type male (XX)

		Gametes from female	
		$\frac{1}{2}X$	$\frac{1}{2}Y^B$
Gametes from male	All X	$\frac{1}{2}XX$	$\frac{1}{2}XY^B$
		Wild type males	Black females

5 *Genes and chromosomes*

51 (a) Dark green, $Bb\, i^1 i^2$; (b) dark green, light green, cobalt and sky blue; (c) dark green and sky blue.

52 In the absence of linkage, the four phenotypic classes should occur in equal proportions, but crimson, flat and pink, inrolled occur at a lower frequency. These have the genotypes $Pp\, Ii$ and $pp\, ii$ respectively. Therefore in the $Pp\, Ii$ which were backcrossed, P and i were on one homologue and p and I were on the other, i.e. $\dfrac{P \quad i}{p \quad I}$.

53 1 cubitus interruptus, eyeless $\dfrac{(ci \quad ey)}{(ci \quad ey)}$: 3 wild type $\dfrac{(Ci\ Ey)}{(ci \quad ey)}, \dfrac{(Ci\ Ey)}{(Ci\ Ey)}$.

54 (a) $\dfrac{Ci \quad ey}{ci \quad Ey}$;

(b) 1 eyeless $\dfrac{(Ci\ ey)}{(Ci\ ey)}$: 2 wild type $\dfrac{(Ci\ ey)}{(ci\ Ey)}$: 1 cubitus interruptus $\dfrac{(ci\ Ey)}{(ci\ Ey)}$.

55 The mother with the nail–patella syndrome carries I^A on the same chromosome. X has inherited the nail–patella syndrome and therefore also has the linked I^A allele (assuming crossing over has not occurred between the loci). She has inherited I^O from her father and is therefore blood group A.

56 (a) Ss;   (b) $\frac{1}{4}$;   (c) $\frac{1}{4}$;   (d) $\frac{1}{4}$.

(e) The parent plants have the genotype $\dfrac{S\ \ G}{s\ \ g}$ If there is no crossing over the progeny will be in the ratio

$$1\,\dfrac{S\ \ G}{S\ \ G}:2\,\dfrac{s\ \ g}{S\ \ G}:1\,\dfrac{s\ \ g}{s\ \ g}$$

3 single, pale green : 1 double, dark green

Commercially produced ten week stocks incorporate a third linked allele which causes death of pollen grains carrying it. This has the effect of increasing the proportion of double flowered plants.

57 (a) Wild type wings, vermilion eyes $\dfrac{Bf\ \ v}{}\rightarrow$

Bifid wings, wild type eyes $\dfrac{bf\ \ V}{}\rightarrow$

Wild type wings and eyes $\dfrac{Bf\ \ V}{}\rightarrow$

Bifid wings, vermilion eyes $\dfrac{bf\ \ v}{}\rightarrow$

(b) Wild type wings and eye colour;   bifid wings and vermilion eyes.

58 (a) Grey, straight, *B/b cu/cu*; cinnamon, curly, *b/b Cu/cu*.

(b) 156·25.

(c) $\chi^2 = 22{\cdot}88$. With 3 degrees of freedom, this is significant at below the 0·001 level of probability.

(d) Grey, curly $\dfrac{B\ \ Cu}{b\ \ cu}$; grey, straight $\dfrac{B\ \ cu}{b\ \ cu}$; cinnamon, curly $\dfrac{b\ \ Cu}{b\ \ cu}$;

cinnamon, straight $\dfrac{b\ \ cu}{b\ \ cu}$.

59 (a) Let *w* be the allele for waltzer and *W* be the wild type allele.

Let *a* be the allele for albino and *A* be the wild type allele.

The parents of the backcross progeny had the genotypes

$\dfrac{A\ \ w}{a\ \ W}$ and $\dfrac{a\ \ w}{a\ \ w}$.

(b) Expected number in each phenotypic class is 95.

60 (a)

	(i)	(ii)
Dark eyed, coloured	326·25	290
Pink eyed, dilute	108·75	145
Albino	145	145

(b) Dark eyed, coloured occur less frequently than expected on the basis of independent assortment and the other two phenotype groups occur more frequently. The observed numbers are closer to the numbers expected if the genes were linked with no crossing over.

(c) Pleiotropic.

61 Linkage is detected through the calculation of recombination frequencies in large samples of offspring from crosses between known genotypes. It is not possible to do such breeding experiments with humans. Recent advances in cytogenetics and recombinant DNA techniques (genetic engineering) are allowing human chromosomes to be mapped by other means.

62 (a) Normal endosperm, normal size 358·3
Normal endosperm, dwarf 119·4
Shrunken endosperm, normal size 119·4
Shrunken endosperm, dwarf 39·8

(b) $\chi^2 = 45\cdot9$. With 3 degrees of freedom, this is significant at below the 0·001 level of probability.

(c) The 'D' and 'Sh' loci are on the same chromosome but some crossing over between them occurs. *D* is on the same homologue as *sh* and *d* is on the same homologue as *Sh*. *D Sh* and *d sh* are recombinant chromosomes and genotypes containing either or both of these are less frequent than expected on the assumption of independent assortment.

63 (a) There is a different phenotypic ratio in the male and female progeny.

(b) Wild type body and eye colour $\dfrac{Y \quad W}{}$

Yellow body, wild type eye $\dfrac{y \quad W}{}$

Wild type body, white eye $\dfrac{Y \quad w}{}$

(c) (i) 1·2:1; (ii) 1:1; (iii) yellow has lower viability than wild type.

(d) (i) Wild type female × yellow bodied, white eyed male.

(ii) Wild type body, white eye; yellow body, wild type eye; wild type body and eye; yellow body, white eye.

(iii) Wild type body and eye, and yellow body, white eye

64 (a) $\dfrac{c^{ch} \quad b \quad y}{c^{h} \quad B \quad Y}$

(b) $\dfrac{c^{h} \quad B \quad Y}{c \quad b \quad y}$ $\dfrac{c^{ch} \quad B \quad Y}{c \quad b \quad y}$

$\dfrac{c^{h} \quad B \quad y}{c \quad b \quad y}$ $\dfrac{c^{ch} \quad B \quad y}{c \quad b \quad y}$

$\dfrac{c^{h} \quad b \quad Y}{c \quad b \quad y}$ $\dfrac{c^{ch} \quad b \quad Y}{c \quad b \quad y}$

$\dfrac{c^{h} \quad b \quad y}{c \quad b \quad y}$ $\dfrac{c^{ch} \quad b \quad y}{c \quad b \quad y}$

(c) $\dfrac{c^{h} \quad B \quad Y}{c \quad b \quad y}$ and $\dfrac{c^{ch} \quad b \quad y}{c \quad b \quad y}$

(d) Ignore the third locus completely; the order of the genes is not known at this stage.

    (i) $7 + 125 + 108 + 16 = 256$

    (ii) $7 + 46 + 55 + 16 = 124$

    (iii) $125 + 46 + 55 + 108 = 334$

(e) The smallest number of recombinations is between 'Y' and 'C', so these are the closest loci.

(f) 'C' and 'B' are furthest apart so 'Y' must be the middle locus.

(g) $\dfrac{c^{ch}\ \ Y\ \ b}{c\ \ \ y\ \ \ b}$ and $\dfrac{c^{h}\ \ y\ \ B}{c\ \ \ y\ \ \ b}$. The genes are given in the correct order. Notice that these genotypes also occur in the lowest frequency.

65 (a) $\dfrac{l\ \ \ r\ \ \ s}{l\ \ \ r\ \ \ s}$ and $\dfrac{L\ \ R\ \ S}{l\ \ \ r\ \ \ s}$

    (b) $\dfrac{156 + 54 + 180 + 39}{3684} = 0{\cdot}116 = 11{\cdot}6\%$

    (c) $\dfrac{54 + 526 + 39 + 634}{3684} = 0{\cdot}34 = 34\%$

    (d) $\dfrac{l\ \ R\ \ s}{l\ \ \ r\ \ \ s}$ and $\dfrac{L\ \ r\ \ S}{l\ \ \ r\ \ \ s}$

6 *Population genetics*

66 (a) Some students find it helpful at first to use the following visual method when answering questions involving the Hardy–Weinberg equation. Start with a Punnett square. Fill in any information given. In this problem we know that

$$q^2 = \frac{1}{10\,000} = 0{\cdot}0001$$

therefore $q = \sqrt{0{\cdot}0001} = 0{\cdot}01$

		Frequency of male gametes	
		$p =$	$q = 0{\cdot}01$
Frequency of female gametes	p	$p^2 =$	$pq =$
	q	$pq =$	$q^2 = 0{\cdot}0001$

$p + q = 1$

$\quad p = 1 - 0{\cdot}01$

$\quad\ \ = 0{\cdot}99$

Add p = 0·99 to the table.

According to the Hardy–Weinberg formula, the frequency of heterozygotes is 2pq.

$$2pq = 2 \times 0·01 \times 0·99$$
$$= 0·0198$$

So about 20 people in 1000 would be expected to be heterozygous.

(b) If a couple have already had one phenylketonuric child, they must both be heterozygous. The probability of two heterozygotes having a heterozygous child is $\frac{1}{2}$.

67 Let q equal the frequency of Fy^b which is given as 0·6. Let p be the frequency of Fy^a.

$$p + q = 1$$
$$p = 1 - q$$
$$= 0·4$$

In the Hardy–Weinberg equation, $p^2 + 2pq + q^2 = 1$,

frequency of $Fy^a/Fy^a = p^2 = 0·4^2 = 0·16$
frequency of $Fy^a/Fy^b = 2pq = 2 \times 0·4 \times 0·6 = 0·48$
frequency of $Fy^b/Fy^b = q^2 = 0·6^2 = 0·36$

68 (a) (i) In the Hardy–Weinberg equation, $p^2 + 2pq + q^2 = 1$, q^2 is the frequency of the homozygous recessive genotype.

$q^2 = \frac{31}{129} = 0·24$

In males q = 0·49.

(ii) $q^2 = \frac{19}{123} = 0·154$

In females q = 0·39.

(b) The samples of males and females are small and the difference in calculated allele frequencies is due to sampling error. Larger samples would allow an estimation of the true allele frequencies to be made and we should expect no difference between males and females.

69 (a) $2·5\% = \dfrac{2·5}{100} = 0·025.$

In the Hardy–Weinberg equation, $p^2 + 2pq + q^2 = 1$,
Frequency of sickle cell anaemia = $q^2 = 0·025$
$$q = \sqrt{0·025}$$
Frequency of Hb^S allele = q = 0·158

(b)
$$p + q = 1$$
$$p = 1 - 0·158$$
Frequency of Hb^A allele = p = 0·842
Frequency of heterozygotes = 2pq = $2 \times 0·842 \times 0·158 = 0·266$
Number of heterozygotes in a population of 500 is $500 \times 0·266 = 133$

70 (a) Let the alleles for feather colour be b^1 and b^2.
Blue × blue gives $\frac{1}{4}$ black, $\frac{1}{2}$ blue and $\frac{1}{4}$ white. $\frac{1}{4} \times 64 = 16$.
16 are expected to be white.

(b) 48 birds remain of which 32 are blue (b^1/b^2) and 16 are black (b^2/b^2)
There are $2 \times 48 = 96$ alleles of which 32 are b^1.
Proportion of b^1 alleles $= \frac{32}{96} = \frac{1}{3} = q$
Proportion of white birds after selection $= q^2 = (\frac{1}{3})^2 = \frac{1}{9} = 0.111$.

71 (a) The mother has genotype *dd*. A child at risk has inherited *D* from the father so the father could be *Dd* or *DD*.

(b) The probability that a rhesus negative woman will marry a rhesus positive man is the same as the frequency of *DD* plus *Dd* in the population (assuming that she does not choose her husband on the basis of his blood group). If the frequency of allele *d* is 0·4, the frequency of allele *D* is $1 - 0.4 = 0.6$. Let $q = 0.4$ and $p = 0.6$. In the Hardy–Weinberg equation $p^2 + 2pq + q^2 = 1$, p^2 is the frequency of *DD* and $2pq$ is the frequency of *Dd*.
$$p^2 = 0.36 \ (DD)$$
$$2pq = 0.48 \ (Dd)$$
The proportion of the population who are either *DD* or *Dd* (the proportion is the same in males and females) is $0.36 + 0.48 = 0.84$. Therefore, the probability that a rhesus negative woman will marry a rhesus positive man is 0·84.

72 (a) There are 352 females so the total number of alleles is $352 \times 2 = 704$.
Total $X^G = (2 \times 15) + 91 = 121$
Total $X^g = 91 + (2 \times 246) = 583$
Frequency $X^G = \frac{121}{704} = 0.17$
Frequency $X^g = \frac{583}{704} = 0.83$

(b) Males have only one X-chromosome and the allele frequency is the same in both sexes. Therefore the proportion of males which are $X^G Y = 0.17$ (and the proportion which are $X^g Y$ is 0·83). Therefore out of 334 males, $0.17 \times 334 = 57$ are ginger.

73 (a) Let $q = 0.1$ (frequency of Hb^S)
Frequency of $Hb^A = p$
$p + q = 1$, therefore $p = 1 - q$
$$p = 0.9$$
Using the Hardy–Weinberg equation $p^2 + 2pq + q^2 = 1$,
$$p^2 = 0.81 \ (Hb^A/Hb^A)$$
$$2pq = 0.18 \ Hb^A/Hb^S)$$
$$q^2 = 0.01 \ (Hb^S/Hb^S)$$
Out of 1000 babies, $1000 \times 0.81 = 810$ are Hb^A/Hb^A,
$1000 \times 0.18 = 180$ are Hb^A/Hb^S,
$1000 \times 0.01 = 10$ are Hb^S/Hb^S.

(b) All of the Hb^S/Hb^S and 20% of the Hb^A/Hb^A die before reproducing so their genes are lost from the gene pool.
20% of $810 = 162$, therefore $810 - 162 = 648 \ Hb^A/Hb^A$ are left, together with 180 Hb^A/Hb^S.

$648 + 180 = 828$ people. Therefore there are $2 \times 828 = 1656$ alleles.
Frequency of Hb^S allele $= \frac{180}{1656} = 0 \cdot 109$

In populations living where malaria is endemic, the allele frequencies remain constant. Sickle cell homozygotes usually die before reproducing, so reducing the number of Hb^S alleles in the gene pool. For allele frequencies to remain constant, an equivalent number of Hb^A alleles are also removed by the death of Hb^A/Hb^A. Problem number 73 demonstrates that to maintain a stable allele frequency of $0 \cdot 1$ for Hb^S, the reproductive rate of Hb^A/Hb^A homozygotes is about 20% less than that of Hb^A/Hb^S heterozygotes.

74 (a) The 51% resistant rats have the genotype RR or Rr. The 49% non-resistant rats have the genotype rr.
In the Hardy–Weinberg equation $p^2 + 2pq + q^2 = 1$, q^2 is the frequency of rr.
$q^2 = 0 \cdot 49$ therefore $q = 0 \cdot 7$
$p + q = 1$, therefore $p = 1 - q$
$$p = 0 \cdot 3$$
Frequency of allele $R = 0 \cdot 3$

(b) $p = 0 \cdot 3$ and $q = 0 \cdot 7$
$p^2 = 0 \cdot 09 \ (RR)$
$2pq = 0 \cdot 42 \ (Rr)$
$q^2 = 0 \cdot 49 \ (rr)$
Out of 100 rats, 9 are RR, 42 are Rr and 49 are rr.

(c) Non-resistant rats have the genotype rr. If all these were killed, there would be 9 RR and 42 Rr rats remaining.
$9 + 42 = 51$ animals remaining. $2 \times 51 = 102$ alleles.
Number of r alleles $= 42$
Frequency of $r = \frac{42}{102} = 0 \cdot 41$
Substitute $q = 0 \cdot 41$ in the Hardy–Weinberg equation
Frequency of non-resistant rats $(rr) = q^2 = 0 \cdot 17$

75 (a) Let the alleles responsible for colouring be d^1 and d^2. The population consists of 158 d^1/d^1, 280 d^1/d^2 and 212 d^2/d^2.
Total number of birds $= 650$. Total number of alleles $= 2 \times 650 = 1300$
Number of d^1 alleles $= (2 \times 158) + 280 = 596$
Number of d^2 alleles $= 280 + (2 \times 212) = 704$
Frequency of $d^1 = \frac{596}{1300} = 0 \cdot 458$
Frequency of $d^2 = \frac{704}{1300} = 0 \cdot 542$
Substitute $p = 0 \cdot 458$ and $q = 0 \cdot 542$ in the Hardy–Weinberg equation, $p^2 + 2pq + q^2 = 1$.
$p^2 = 0 \cdot 21 \ (d^1/d^1)$
$2pq = 0 \cdot 50 \ (d^1/d^2)$
$q^2 = 0 \cdot 29 \ (d^2/d^2)$

Expected number of $d^1/d^1 = 0.21 \times 650 = 136.5$ (pale)

$$d^1/d^2 = 0.50 \times 650 = 325 \text{ (intermediate)}$$
$$d^2/d^2 = 0.29 \times 650 = 188.5 \text{ (dark)}$$

(b) $\chi^2 = 12.55$. This is significant at below the 0.01 level of probability.

(c) To assess the biological significance of the departure of observed numbers from expected numbers, we must look at the nature of the deviation. There are fewer heterozygotes and more homozygotes than expected. An excess of homozygotes suggests that similar genotypes are breeding with each other, i.e. there is non-random mating. If birds tend to choose mates of a similar colour to themselves, pale and dark birds will have only pale and dark offspring respectively. Only half of the offspring of intermediate birds will be intermediate. This will lead to a deficiency of intermediates when observed numbers are compared with numbers expected on the basis of the Hardy–Weinberg equilibrium.

Answers to tests

Test A

A1 (a) Short, homozygous recessive (e.g. *tt*); tall A, heterozygous (e.g. *Tt*); tall B, homozygous dominant (e.g. *TT*)
  (b) 36

A2 Secretors produce a non-secretor so the two secretor parents must be heterozygous. They show the effects of the dominant allele.

A3 (a) 50% green and 50% golden
  (b) No. Green × white cannot be crossed because plants lacking chlorophyll die as seedlings

A4 One-quarter

Test B

B1 C

B2 (a) The allele for rough hair.
  (b) Rough haired (*Rr*) × smooth haired (*rr*). Litter are *Rr* and *rr*.

B3 (a) *Ll Dd*, white.
  (b) (i) 1 *Ll Dd* : 1 *Ll dd* : 1 *ll Dd* : 1 *ll dd*; (ii) 3 white : 1 coloured

B4 (a) Comice; (b) one-quarter; (c) three-eighths; (d) 8

Test C

C1 (a) $\frac{1}{16}$
  (b) Short haired black and short haired Siamese.
  (c) *Cc Ll* or *cc Ll* (*C* – black, *c* – Siamese, *L* – short hair, *l* – long hair).
  (d) Cross *cc Ll* × *cc Ll*. One-quarter of the progeny are expected to be Persian-Siamese.

C2 (a) One-quarter; (b) $\frac{9}{16}$; (c) $\frac{3}{32}$

C3 (a) 9 bay : 3 black : 4 chestnut

(b) *B* and *I* together produce bay. *bb* is epistatic to the 'I' locus and produces chestnut. *ii* is epistatic to *B* and gives black.

C4 (a) Let the alleles controlling broad petals or star shape be p^1 and p^2. Let the allele for flat flowers be *F* and the allele for funnel flowers be *f*. The phenotype of the parents is 'fimbriata', flat and the genotype is $p^1 p^2 Ff$.

(b) Broad, flat $p^1 p^1 FF$ or $p^1 p^1 Ff$

Broad, funnel $p^1 p^1 ff$

'Cuspidata' flat $p^2 p^2 FF$ or $p^2 p^2 Ff$

'Cuspidata', funnel $p^2 p^2 ff$

'Fimbriata', flat $p^1 p^2 FF$ or $p^1 p^2 Ff$

'Fimbriata', funnel $p^1 p^2 ff$

Test D

D1 Let the allele for haemophilia be *h* and the allele for normal blood be *H*. Let the allele for colour-blindness be *c* and the allele for normal vision be *C*. The woman's father was $X_C^h Y$. The woman must have inherited *H* and *c* from her mother as she is not a haemophiliac and has a colour-blind son. She must be $X_C^h X_c^H$. Crossing over can occur between 'H' and 'C' during meiosis in the woman so she can produce four types of gametes, X_C^h, X_c^H, X_c^h and X_C^H. Sons will result when these are fertilized by Y-bearing sperm. The first son is $X_c^H Y$ and the second son is $X_C^H Y$.

D2 (a) Black *Bb Ee*, liver brown *bb Ee*;   (b) black *BB Ee*;   (c) 1 black : 1 liver brown : 1 red : 1 yellow.

D3 $\frac{2}{3}$.

D4 (a) One.

(b) Stock A *W/W*; stock B w^s/w^s; stock C, w^n/w^n.

(c) The alleles w^s and w^n are both recessive to *W* but are incompletely dominant to each other.

Test E

E1 (a) One-quarter; (b) one-quarter.

E2 Recombinants (starchy, liguleless and sugary, normal) constitute about 50% of the total so there is no evidence of linkage. The reason that a 1 : 1 : 1 : 1 ratio is not obtained is that there is a deficiency of sugary seeds. As the seeds must be grown in order to determine the leaf character, perhaps the sugary seeds do not germinate as well as the starchy ones.

E3 (a) Striped female × greasy male

$X^{Ta} X^{ta}$ $X^{Ta} Y$

		Gametes from male	
		X^{Ta}	Y
Gametes from female	X^{Ta}	$X^{Ta} X^{Ta}$	$X^{Ta} Y$
	X^{ta}	$X^{Ta} X^{ta}$	$X^{ta} Y$

Expected offspring are 1 greasy male : 1 normal male : 1 greasy female : 1 tabby female.

(b) $X^{ta} X^{ta}$ × $X^{Ta} Y$
↓
$X^{Ta} X^{ta}$ × $X^{Ta} Y$
↓
$X^{Ta} X^{Ta}$ (greasy females)

E4 (a) Let one stock be *AA bb* and the other be *aa BB* where *aa* and *bb* both produce red eyes regardless of the genotype at the other locus. The F_1 shrimps are *Aa Bb* and have black eyes because they are homozygous recessive at neither locus.

(b) *AA bb, Aa bb, aa BB, aa Bb* and *aa bb*.

Test F

F1 (a) Frequency of $L^M = 0{\cdot}64$; frequency of $L^N = 0{\cdot}36$.

(b) Expected numbers are approximately: group M, 87; group MN, 98; group N, 28. These are close to the observed numbers so the population is in Hardy–Weinberg equilibrium.

F2 (a) 9 black : 3 red : 4 white

(b) Let the loci be 'C' and 'D'. The black eyed F_1 flies are *Cc Dd*. The presence of at least one dominant allele at each locus gives black eyes. One of the loci, say 'C', gives white when homozygous recessive and is epistatic to the 'D' locus so *cc DD*, *cc Dd* and *cc dd* are white eyed. *Cc dd* and *CC dd* are red eyed.

(c) White eyed female, *cc Dd*; red eyed male, *CC dd*.

F3 The recombinants occur in the lowest frequencies. Allele *a* is more often found with *we* than with *We*. Allele *a'* is more often found with *We* than with *we*. Allele *B* is found equally frequently with *a*, *a'*, *We* and *we*, therefore *a'/a* is linked to *We/we* and *B/b* is not on the same chromosome.

F4 (a) The three types of coat colour are the result of variation at a single gene locus with incomplete dominance. The heterozygote is blue merle.

(b) (i) The alleles controlling coat colour have a pleiotropic effect on eye colour.

(ii) There are two very closely linked genes, one affecting eye colour and the other affecting coat colour. There is incomplete dominance at both gene loci.

Test G

G1 (a) Recessive. (b) The F_2 plants occur in a $3:1$ ratio. (c) $\dfrac{a \quad Er}{A \quad er}$.

G2 (a)

	Banded	Unbanded	Total
Pink	76	245	321
Yellow	370	35	405
Total	446	280	726

   (b) (i) $C^Y/C^Y = \frac{405}{726} = 0.56$. Frequency of $C^Y = 0.75$; frequency of $C^P = 0.25$.

   (ii) $b/b = \frac{446}{726} = 0.61$. Frequency of $b = 0.78$; frequency of $B = 0.22$.

G3 (a) 3 horned : 1 hornless; (b) 3 hornless : 1 horned. (This is similar to the example of balding in humans given in section 4.1.)

G4 (a) Black $\times$ albino gives the required genotype $Aa\ Cc$, for the F_1 generation. When interbred, these produce the required offspring.
   (b) Two-thirds.

Test H

H1 51%.

H2 There is no evidence for linkage. Although the data do not fit a $1:1:1:1$ ratio, a good fit is not expected with such a small sample. In addition, recombinants are in excess of parentals, not less frequent as would be expected if the genes were linked.

H3 This is an example of gene complementation (section 3.4). Gillet's rabbits are homozygous for a recessive allele causing the rex phenotype. Du Bary's rabbits are homozygous recessive at a different gene locus having the same phenotypic effect. The F_1 rabbits have one dominant wild type allele at each of the two loci and so have normal hair.

H4 The pedigrees show that the allele for G6PD deficiency is sex linked and recessive. 10% of males are G6PD deficient, so 10% of X-chromosomes in this population carry the recessive allele. The frequency of G6PD females is $0.1^2 = 0.01 = 1\%$. (See also problem 72.)

Appendix

Table of chi-square values

Degrees of freedom	Probability													
	0·99	0·98	0·95	0·90	0·80	0·70	0·50	0·30	0·20	0·10	0·05	0·02	0·01	0·001
1	0·00016	0·00063	0·0039	0·016	0·064	0·15	0·46	1·07	1·64	2·71	3·84	5·41	6·64	10·83
2	0·02	0·04	0·10	0·21	0·45	0·71	1·39	2·41	3·22	4·60	5·99	7·82	9·21	13·82
3	0·12	0·18	0·35	0·58	1·00	1·42	2·37	3·66	4·64	6·25	7·82	9·84	11·34	16·27
4	0·30	0·43	0·71	1·06	1·65	2·20	3·36	4·88	5·99	7·78	9·49	11·67	13·28	18·46
5	0·55	0·75	1·14	1·61	2·34	3·00	4·35	6·06	7·29	9·24	11·07	13·39	15·09	20·52
6	0·87	1·13	1·64	2·20	3·07	3·83	5·35	7·23	8·56	10·64	12·59	15·03	16·81	22·46
7	1·24	1·56	2·17	2·83	3·82	4·67	6·35	8·38	9·80	12·02	14·07	16·62	18·48	24·32
8	1·65	2·03	2·73	3·49	4·59	5·53	7·34	9·52	11·03	13·36	15·51	18·17	20·09	26·12
9	2·09	2·53	3·32	4·17	5·38	6·39	8·34	10·66	12·24	14·68	16·92	19·68	21·67	27·88
10	2·56	3·06	3·94	4·86	6·18	7·27	9·34	11·78	13·44	15·99	18·31	21·16	23·21	29·59
11	3·05	3·61	4·58	5·58	6·99	8·15	10·34	12·90	14·63	17·28	19·68	22·62	24·72	31·26
12	3·57	4·18	5·23	6·30	7·81	9·03	11·34	14·01	15·81	18·55	21·03	24·05	26·22	32·91
13	4·11	4·76	5·89	7·04	8·63	9·93	12·34	15·12	16·98	19·81	22·36	25·47	27·69	34·53
14	4·66	5·37	6·57	7·79	9·47	10·82	13·34	16·22	18·15	21·06	23·68	26·87	29·14	36·12
15	5·23	5·98	7·26	8·55	10·31	11·72	14·34	17·32	19·31	22·31	25·00	28·26	30·58	37·70
16	5·81	6·61	7·96	9·31	11·15	12·62	15·34	18·42	20·46	23·54	26·30	29·63	32·00	39·25
17	6·41	7·26	8·67	10·08	12·00	13·53	16·34	19·51	21·62	24·77	27·59	31·00	33·41	40·79
18	7·02	7·91	9·39	10·86	12·86	14·44	17·34	20·60	22·76	25·99	28·87	32·35	34·80	42·31
19	7·63	8·57	10·12	11·65	13·72	15·35	18·34	21·69	23·90	27·20	30·14	33·69	36·19	43·82
20	8·26	9·24	10·85	12·44	14·58	16·27	19·34	22·78	25·04	28·41	31·41	35·02	37·57	45·32
21	8·90	9·92	11·59	13·24	15·44	17·18	20·34	23·86	26·17	29·62	32·67	36·34	38·93	46·80
22	9·54	10·60	12·34	14·04	16·31	18·10	21·24	24·94	27·30	30·81	33·92	37·66	40·29	48·27
23	10·20	11·29	13·09	14·85	17·19	19·02	22·34	26·02	28·43	32·01	35·17	38·97	41·64	49·73
24	10·86	11·99	13·85	15·66	18·06	19·94	23·34	27·10	29·55	33·20	36·42	40·27	42·98	51·18
25	11·52	12·70	14·61	16·47	18·94	20·87	24·34	28·17	30·67	34·38	37·65	41·57	44·31	52·62
26	12·20	13·41	15·38	17·29	19·82	21·79	25·34	29·25	31·80	35·56	38·88	42·86	45·64	54·05
27	12·88	14·12	16·15	18·11	20·70	22·72	26·34	30·32	32·91	36·74	40·11	44·14	46·96	55·48
28	13·56	14·85	16·93	18·94	21·59	23·65	27·34	31·39	34·03	37·92	41·34	45·42	48·28	56·89
29	14·26	15·57	17·71	19·77	22·48	24·58	28·34	32·46	35·14	39·09	42·56	46·69	49·59	58·30
30	14·95	16·31	18·49	20·60	23·36	25·51	29·34	33·53	36·25	40·26	43·77	47·96	50·89	59·70

Index